The Menstrual Symphony

Unlocking the Secrets of Hormonal Health

VIDHYA SHANMUGAM

BLUEROSE PUBLISHERS
India | U.K.

Copyright © Vidhya Shanmugam 2024

All rights reserved by author. No part of this publication may be reproduced, stored in a retrieval system or transmitted in any form or by any means, electronic, mechanical, photocopying, recording or otherwise, without the prior permission of the author. Although every precaution has been taken to verify the accuracy of the information contained herein, the publisher assumes no responsibility for any errors or omissions. No liability is assumed for damages that may result from the use of information contained within.

BlueRose Publishers takes no responsibility for any damages, losses, or liabilities that may arise from the use or misuse of the information, products, or services provided in this publication.

For permissions requests or inquiries regarding this publication,
please contact:

BLUEROSE PUBLISHERS
www.BlueRoseONE.com
info@bluerosepublishers.com
+91 8882 898 898
+4407342408967

ISBN: 978-93-93384-91-1

Cover design: Muskan Sachdeva
Typesetting: Pooja Sharma

First Edition: January 2024

Disclaimer:

The information and practices shared in this book, "The Menstrual Symphony," are intended to provide holistic guidance for promoting a healthy menstrual period. However, individual experiences may vary, and it is essential to consult with a qualified healthcare professional for personalized advice based on your specific needs and medical history.

"The Holistic Menstrual Guide For Women: A Comprehensive Guide To Understanding Your Menstrual Cycle, Natural Remedies, and Holistic Practices For Optimal Health And Well-Being"

Vidhya Shanmugam

Why I Wrote This Book

As a women's wellness coach, I am thrilled to share with you the inspiration behind this book. My goal was simple yet powerful: to empower women everywhere to take charge of their health and well-being by harnessing the power of menstrual cycle.

Having experienced firsthand the transformative benefits of aligning my lifestyle with my menstrual cycle, I knew I had to share this knowledge with others. That's why I created a comprehensive guide that covers everything from the basics of menstrual cycle phases to more advanced topics such as Ayurvedic daily practices, yoga, and eating according to your hormones.

In my book, you'll discover how to cultivate cycle aware nutrition that nourishes your body and mind during each phase of your cycle. You'll also learn how to optimize your fitness routine to support your menstrual cycle and unlock your body's full potential. And, of course, sexual wellness and hormone health are essential topics that are also covered in detail.

This book is everything a woman needs to achieve balance and harmony in their lives, using menstrual cycle as a tool to guide them. By sharing the knowledge I gained through personal experience and research, I hope to help other women benefit from this powerful approach.

So, whether you're new to the concept of cycle syncing or are already well-versed in the practice, my book is the perfect resource to help you live a more balanced and harmonious existence. With the tools and information that I will be sharing, you'll be able to make educated decisions about your menstrual cycle and take control of your health and well-being.

Vidhya Shanmugam

Women's Wellness Coach

Contents

Chapter 1: Preparing For Change: Understanding the Cycle   1

Chapter 2: The Hormonal Symphony: Understanding the Key Players in Menstrual Health   9

Chapter 3: Empowering Your Cycle: Fitness for Every Phase   22

Chapter 4: Nourishing Balance: Diet Tips for the Cycle phases   33

Chapter 5: Menstrual Health and Sexual Wellness: Understanding the Connection and Enhancing Your Pleasure   53

Chapter 6: Fertility Awareness Method: Tracking Your Cycle for Birth Control and Pregnancy   61

Chapter 7: Rejuvenating For Renewal: Yoga for Post-Menstrual Recovery   71

Chapter 8: Managing Pain and Discomfort: Natural Remedies for Menstrual Cramps   79

Chapter 9: Hormone Disruptors in Young Women: The Impact of Modern Lifestyle Practices   99

Chapter 10: Embracing The Journey: Celebrating Your Femininity   111

Chapter 11: Recipes   121

Chapter 12: 28 Day Smoothie Recipes   133

About The Author   157

Chapter 1

Preparing For Change: Understanding the Cycle

Let's talk about that time of the month the menstrual cycle. It can be a bit of a mystery, right? Well, I would like to break down the basics of the menstrual cycle and why it's so important to understand it.

We'll dive into the different phases of the cycle and how they affect your hormones, the average length of a cycle, and why it can vary from woman to woman. And don't worry, I won't leave you hanging; I'll explain all about the key hormones involved, like estrogen, progesterone, luteinizing hormone, and follicle - stimulating hormone.

We'll talk about how understanding your menstrual cycle can benefit you in so many ways. From managing those pesky symptoms like bloating, cramps, and mood swings, to optimizing your fitness routine and enhancing your sexual wellness.

We'll tackle those old-school ideas about periods being dirty or shameful and remind you how important self-care and menstrual hygiene really are. And forget about those weird rumors about menstrual blood being unnatural or toxic; we're all about celebrating the natural processes of our amazing female bodies.

So, by the end of this chapter, you'll be a total boss when it comes to understanding your menstrual cycle. You'll have all the tools and information you need to be cycle-aware and ready for whatever each phase brings.

The Four Phases

Women's health is a complicated and ever evolving topic, and knowing the many phases of a woman's cycle is critical to understanding her overall health.

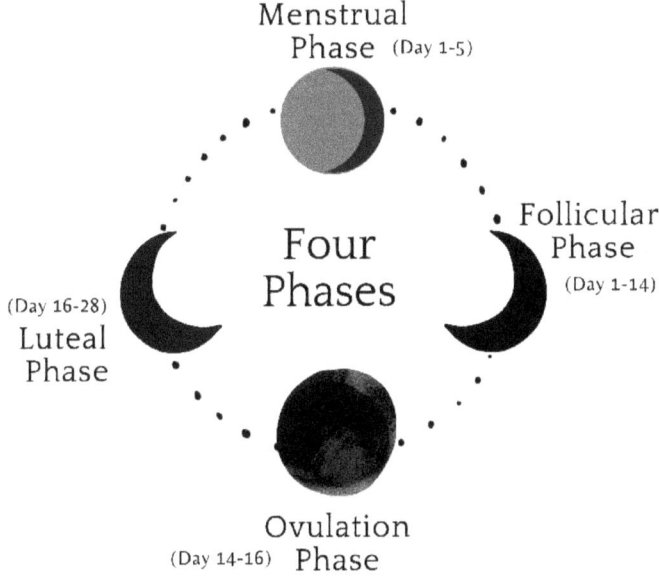

Your cycle isn't just one long period; it's actually broken up into four distinct phases, each with its own hormonal changes and effects on your body. Think of it like a four-act play, with each act bringing something new to the table.

First up is the menstrual phase. This is when you're on your period and lasts about 3-5 days. During this time, your body is preparing for ovulation by releasing hormones like estrogen and progesterone. This shedding of the uterine lining can come with some not-so-fun physical symptoms like cramps, bloating, headaches, and fatigue.

Next is the follicular phase. This phase starts right after your period ends and goes until the day before ovulation. During this phase, your body ramps up production of hormones like estrogen and follicle-stimulating hormone (FSH), which help develop ovarian follicles containing immature eggs. The endometrium, or lining of the uterus, also thickens in preparation for the implantation of a fertilized egg. The follicular phase usually lasts around 14 days and is the longest phase of the menstrual cycle.

Now we move onto the ovulation phase. This is when a mature egg is released from the ovary and travels down the fallopian tube. It usually happens around the middle of your cycle and is the most fertile time for you. Your cervical mucus becomes thinner and clearer during this phase, making it easier for sperm to swim through. You might also experience changes like increased sex drive and breast tenderness, all thanks to rising levels of estrogen and progesterone. If the egg is fertilized, it will implant itself in the uterus, leading to pregnancy.

Finally, we have the luteal phase. This is a crucial period for hormonal changes that affect ovulation and the development of the endometrium in preparation for implantation. Progesterone is secreted from the corpus luteum, a temporary endocrine organ that forms from the ovarian follicle after ovulation. This hormone causes the endometrium to thicken and become more vascularized and increases the production of nutrients that nurture the implanting embryo. The luteal phase also plays an important role in fertility, so it's important that it's of sufficient length and quality for implantation to occur.

During the luteal phase, progesterone levels are high and estrogen levels are low, which can lead to a variety of physical and emotional symptoms like bloating, breast tenderness, irritability, mood swings, fatigue, and difficulty sleeping. Eating a balanced diet, exercising regularly, getting plenty of rest, and avoiding triggers that worsen symptoms can help manage these symptoms. Additionally, taking supplements like magnesium, omega-3 fatty acids, and vitamin B6 can help balance hormones and improve PMS symptoms.

Each of the four phases of the cycle brings with it unique changes in mood, behavior, and personality. What if they are embodied as unique characters?

Follicular Phase:

Character Name: Maya

Personality Description: Maya is a go-getter, always on the move, and full of energy. She is excited about new beginnings and loves to take on challenges. She is confident, creative, and has a strong sense of purpose. During the follicular phase, Maya is at her most optimistic and driven. She is focused on achieving her goals and is always looking for ways to improve herself.

Ovulatory Phase:

Character Name: Leela

Personality Description: Leela is a social butterfly, always surrounded by friends and loved ones. She is warm, friendly, and outgoing, with a magnetic personality that draws people to her. During the ovulatory phase, Leela is at her most vibrant and attractive. She exudes confidence and sex appeal and is in touch with her sensuality. She enjoys exploring new experiences and is open to trying new things.

Luteal Phase:

Character Name: Ava

Personality Description: Ava is a sensitive and nurturing soul. She is compassionate, empathetic, and always there for her friends and family. During the luteal phase, Ava is at her most introspective and reflective. She is in tune with her emotions and may experience mood swings and heightened sensitivity. She takes time to care for herself and focuses on self-care and self-love.

Menstrual Phase:

Character Name: Bhumi

Personality Description: Bhumi is a calming and grounding presence. She is wise, intuitive, and has a deep connection to her inner self. She takes time to slow down, rest, and recharge. She may experience physical discomfort during this phase but is able to stay centered and focused on her inner strength.

Enhancing Fitness and Sexual Wellness

Understanding your menstrual cycle can be a game-changer when it comes to taking care of your body and living your best life.

First off, let's tackle those pesky menstrual symptoms. We've all experienced bloating, cramps, and mood swings during our periods. But did you know that these symptoms can actually be managed and even minimized by understanding your menstrual cycle? By tracking your cycle, you can anticipate when these symptoms might occur and take steps to mitigate them. Whether it's through gentle exercise, stress reduction techniques, or dietary changes, there are so many ways to make your menstrual experience more comfortable.

During different phases of your cycle, your energy levels, strength, and endurance can vary. By understanding these fluctuations, you can optimize your workouts to get the most out of each phase. Whether you're a gym rat or a yoga enthusiast, tailoring your fitness routine to your menstrual cycle can take your workout game to the next level.

Understanding your menstrual cycle can also enhance your sex life. During the ovulatory phase, for example, your libido may be heightened and your body may be more receptive to pleasure. By tracking your cycle and communicating with your partner, you can take advantage of these natural rhythms and experience a more satisfying and fulfilling sex life.

Embracing Menstruation as a Natural Process

For far too long, women have been made to feel ashamed and embarrassed about their menstrual cycle. It's time to throw those old-school ideas out the window and embrace the natural and amazing process that is menstruation. It's not dirty or shameful, it's a beautiful and necessary part of being a woman.

Self-care is crucial during your menstrual cycle. Your body is going through a lot, and it's important to take care of yourself both physically and mentally. This means taking time for rest and relaxation, eating healthy foods, and practicing self-love. And let's not forget about menstrual hygiene. Proper hygiene is essential for maintaining good health and preventing infections. Using the right products and changing them regularly is key to staying fresh and clean.

There are some strange rumors out there about menstrual blood being unnatural or toxic, but this couldn't be further from the truth. Menstrual blood is a natural bodily fluid, just like sweat or saliva. It's not toxic or dirty, it's a perfectly normal part of the female reproductive process.

So let's celebrate our bodies and the incredible things they can do. Don't let old myths and rumors hold you back from embracing your menstrual cycle. Take care of yourself, practice good hygiene, and remember that menstruation is a natural and beautiful part of being a woman.

Chapter 2

The Hormonal Symphony: Understanding the Key Players in Menstrual Health

As a women's health coach, I understand the importance of hormonal balance in achieving optimal menstrual health. Hormones are like the instruments in an orchestra, each playing a unique role in the beautiful symphony of our bodies. We will explore the key hormones that play a significant role in menstrual health, including estrogen, progesterone, testosterone, follicle-stimulating hormone (FSH), luteinizing hormone (LH), prolactin, thyroid hormones, and cortisol.

We will delve into the functions of each hormone, the effects of imbalances, and practical ways to achieve hormonal balance through a holistic approach. Understanding the role of each hormone and how they work together will empower you to take control of your menstrual health and improve your overall well - being.

Firstly, Estrogen, the hormone responsible for the development and regulation of the female reproductive system, We will discuss the types of estrogen, the effects of an imbalance, and natural ways to balance estrogen levels. Progesterone is the hormone responsible for preparing the body for pregnancy. In addition, we will discuss testosterone, the hormone primarily associated with male reproductive health but also important for women's health.

Furthermore, we will dive into the roles of FSH and LH in menstrual health, as well as prolactin, the hormone responsible for lactation. We will also discuss thyroid hormones, which are crucial for regulating metabolism and energy levels, and cortisol, the stress hormone.

We will conclude with the importance of understanding and balancing hormones for optimal menstrual health. We will explore holistic approaches to achieving hormonal balance, including nutrition, exercise, and stress management. You will have a comprehensive understanding of the hormonal symphony that plays a significant role in menstrual health and practical ways to achieve balance for optimal well-being.

Estrogen

Estrogen is one of the primary female sex hormones that plays a vital role in the development and regulation of the female reproductive system. It is responsible for the growth and maintenance of the uterus and fallopian tubes, as well as the development of secondary sex characteristics such as breasts and pubic hair. Most of the Estrogen is produced from ovaries and small amounts from our adrenal glands and fat cells.

There are three main types of estrogen: estrone (E1), estradiol (E2), and estriol (E3). Estradiol is the most abundant and potent type of estrogen, and is responsible for most of the physiological effects of estrogen in the body.

An imbalance in estrogen levels can lead to a range of symptoms, including irregular periods, mood swings, weight gain, and hot flashes. It can also increase the risk of certain health conditions, such as breast cancer, endometriosis, and osteoporosis.

Fortunately, there are many natural ways to balance estrogen levels. Eating a balanced diet rich in fruits, vegetables, and whole grains can help support healthy estrogen levels. Certain foods, such as flaxseeds, soy products, and cruciferous vegetables like broccoli contain compounds that can help regulate estrogen levels.

Regular exercise can also help balance estrogen levels, as can reducing stress through practices like meditation, yoga, or deep breathing exercises. Certain supplements, such as omega-3 fatty acids, vitamin D, and magnesium, can also support healthy estrogen levels.

Overall, understanding the functions of estrogen, the different types of estrogen, the effects of an imbalance, and natural ways to balance estrogen levels is crucial for maintaining optimal menstrual health. By taking a holistic approach to hormonal balance, we can help support our bodies and achieve a more balanced and harmonious hormonal symphony.

I would match this outline to the character of Katniss Everdeen, portrayed by Jennifer Lawrence, in "The Hunger Games" movie series.

Katniss, as a female character, embodies the strength and resilience associated with estrogen. She is a symbol of female power and determination, much like the role of estrogen in the female body. Katniss is also a fighter, much like the role of estrogen in protecting the female reproductive system from harm.

Moreover, the concept of balance is crucial to Katniss' character arc throughout the movies. She learns to balance her survival instincts with her compassion for others, just as it is important to balance estrogen levels for optimal health. She also learns the importance of taking a holistic approach to life, just as the outline suggests taking a holistic approach to hormonal balance.

Overall, Katniss Everdeen is a fitting match for this outline due to her embodiment of female strength and resilience, her journey towards balance, and her representation of the importance of taking a holistic approach to life.

Progesterone

Progesterone is a crucial hormone for women's health and plays an essential role in preparing the body for pregnancy. It is produced by the ovaries and the adrenal glands and is involved in regulating the menstrual cycle.

The primary function of progesterone is to prepare the uterus for implantation of a fertilized egg. It helps thicken the lining of the uterus and creates a hospitable environment for the embryo to grow. If fertilization doesn't occur, progesterone levels drop, signaling the body to shed the uterine lining and start a new menstrual cycle.

An imbalance in progesterone levels can cause a range of symptoms, such as irregular periods, heavy bleeding, mood swings, and infertility. Low progesterone levels can also lead to an increased risk of miscarriage, as the uterus may not be able to support a pregnancy.

Fortunately, there are natural ways to balance progesterone levels. One way is to incorporate progesterone-rich foods into your diet, such as nuts and seeds. These foods contain high levels of zinc, which is essential for progesterone production.

Another way to balance progesterone levels is to reduce stress levels. When the body is under stress, it produces cortisol, which can interfere with progesterone production. Practices like meditation, yoga, and deep breathing can help reduce stress and promote relaxation.

Additionally, certain herbs and supplements can help balance progesterone levels. For example, chasteberry, also known as vitex, is an herb that has been used for centuries to support female reproductive health. It helps to balance hormones by increasing progesterone levels and reducing levels of the follicle - stimulating hormone (FSH).

Progesterone is a vital hormone for women's health, and balancing its levels is essential for a healthy menstrual cycle and optimal fertility. Incorporating progesterone-rich foods, reducing stress levels, and using natural supplements can help support progesterone production and maintain hormonal balance.

I would match this outline to the character of Joy, played by Jennifer Lawrence in the movie "Joy"

Joy is a strong, determined woman who becomes a successful entrepreneur by inventing a self-wringing mop. Her journey to success is filled with obstacles and setbacks, but she never gives up on her dreams. In many ways, her story parallels the importance of progesterone in women's health.

Just as Joy had to overcome challenges and setbacks to achieve her goals, women need to balance their progesterone levels to maintain a healthy menstrual cycle and fertility. The importance of progesterone in preparing the uterus for pregnancy is similar to Joy's determination to create a successful business. Both require a strong foundation and a hospitable environment to grow and thrive.

Additionally, just as Joy had to incorporate new ideas and methods to improve her product, women can balance their progesterone levels by incorporating progesterone-rich foods and natural supplements into their diet. Finally, Joy's ability to reduce stress and stay focused on her goals is similar to the importance of stress reduction in maintaining hormonal balance.

Overall, I chose Joy as a match for this outline because her story embodies the determination, perseverance, and resilience that women need to balance their progesterone levels and maintain optimal reproductive health.

Testosterone

Testosterone is often thought of as a hormone that is exclusively important for men's health, but did you know that it also plays a crucial role in women's reproductive and overall health? We'll take a deep dive into the functions of testosterone, what happens when there is an imbalance, and how to balance testosterone levels for optimal health.

Testosterone is primarily produced in the ovaries and adrenal glands and is involved in the growth and maintenance of reproductive tissues, such as the ovaries and uterus. It also plays a key role in bone health, muscle mass, and overall energy levels. Additionally, testosterone is important for a woman's libido and sexual function.

However, when there is an imbalance in testosterone levels, it can lead to a range of symptoms and health issues. High levels of testosterone in women, also known as hyperandrogenism, can lead to acne, excessive hair growth, and menstrual irregularities. Conversely, low levels of testosterone, also known as hypogonadism, can cause decreased libido, fatigue, and decreased muscle mass and bone density.

So, how can we balance testosterone levels for optimal health? One way is through lifestyle changes such as exercise, stress management, and a healthy diet. Resistance training, for example, has been shown to increase testosterone levels in women. Additionally, certain foods such as avocado, nuts, contain nutrients that can support healthy testosterone production.

There are also medical interventions that can help balance testosterone levels, such as hormone replacement therapy (HRT) or medications that block the production of testosterone. However, it's important to work with a healthcare provider to determine the best course of action based on your individual needs and health history.

I would match this outline to the character of Wonder Woman, portrayed by Gal Gadot in the movie "Wonder Woman."

Wonder Woman is a strong, independent female character who embodies many of the traits associated with balanced testosterone levels, such as strength, energy, and sexual vitality. Additionally, her physical abilities and muscular physique are indicative of the importance of testosterone in maintaining muscle mass and bone density.

Furthermore, Wonder Woman's character is a great example of how women can be both feminine and powerful, and how the balance of hormones in the body is important for overall health and wellbeing. She also highlights the importance of taking care of oneself through exercise and healthy habits to maintain optimal health.

FSH and LH

FSH and LH are two essential hormones that play a crucial role in the menstrual cycle. FSH, or follicle-stimulating hormone, is produced by the pituitary gland and is responsible for the growth and development of ovarian follicles in the ovary. This hormone is crucial for the process of ovulation, as it helps stimulate the growth of the follicles that will eventually release the egg. Without FSH, the menstrual cycle cannot proceed as normal.

An imbalance of FSH levels can lead to irregular periods, anovulation, and difficulty getting pregnant. In some cases, high levels of FSH can indicate a decrease in ovarian reserve, which can make it more difficult to conceive. However, there are several ways to balance FSH levels and promote hormonal health. Some natural remedies include maintaining a healthy diet, reducing stress, and incorporating regular exercise into your routine.

LH, or luteinizing hormone, is another important hormone that is responsible for triggering ovulation. This hormone works in conjunction with FSH to regulate the menstrual cycle and ensure that ovulation occurs at the proper time. LH levels typically surge just before ovulation, signaling the release of the mature egg from the ovary.

An imbalance of LH levels can lead to irregular periods, anovulation, and difficulty getting pregnant. High levels of LH may indicate a condition known as polycystic ovary syndrome (PCOS), which can cause hormonal imbalances and difficulty conceiving.

Overall, FSH and LH are two of the key hormones that play a critical role in menstrual health. Understanding the functions of these hormones, as well as the effects of an imbalance, is essential for achieving optimal hormonal health and reproductive function.

I would match this outline to the character of Miranda Priestly, played by Meryl Streep, in the movie "The Devil Wears Prada." Miranda Priestly is a powerful and highly successful magazine editor who is known for her perfectionism and demanding nature. She is always in control, and her precise attention to detail ensures that her magazine is always on the cutting edge.

Just like FSH and LH are crucial for the menstrual cycle and reproductive health, Miranda Priestly is essential for the success of her magazine. Her strict leadership style and attention to detail are necessary to ensure that the magazine runs smoothly and produces the highest quality content.

Moreover, Miranda's character shows how an imbalance can lead to negative consequences, such as when her personal life becomes affected due to her professional ambitions. Similarly, an imbalance of FSH and LH levels can lead to irregular periods, anovulation, and difficulty conceiving.

Finally, just like how natural remedies and medical guidance can help balance FSH and LH levels, Miranda Priestly's character shows the importance of finding balance in one's personal and professional lives to achieve overall well-being.

Prolactin

Prolactin is a hormone produced by the pituitary gland that plays an important role in lactation and breast development. It is also involved in the regulation of the menstrual cycle and plays a role in mood and behavior. When prolactin levels are too high, it can lead to irregular periods, infertility, and reduced or delayed breast milk production in women who are not breastfeeding. In men, high prolactin levels can cause erectile dysfunction and decreased libido.

One of the most common causes of high prolactin levels is a benign tumor on the pituitary gland called a prolactinoma. Other causes may include certain medications, hypothyroidism, and chronic stress. To balance prolactin levels, it is important to address the underlying cause. Treatment may include medication to reduce prolactin levels, hormone replacement therapy, or lifestyle changes such as reducing stress and getting regular exercise.

Thyroid Hormones

The thyroid gland produces hormones that play a key role in regulating metabolism, energy production, and growth and development. When thyroid hormone levels are too low (hypothyroidism), it can lead to fatigue, weight gain, depression, and irregular periods. When thyroid hormone levels are too high (hyperthyroidism), it can lead to anxiety, weight loss, and irregular periods.

Thyroid hormone imbalances can be caused by a variety of factors, including autoimmune disorders, nutrient deficiencies, and stress. Treatment for thyroid hormone imbalances depends on the underlying cause and may include medication, dietary changes, and lifestyle modifications such as stress reduction techniques and regular exercise.

Cortisol

Cortisol is a hormone produced by the adrenal glands in response to stress. It plays a key role in regulating blood sugar levels, blood pressure, and immune function. When cortisol levels are too high, it can lead to anxiety, insomnia, and irregular periods. When cortisol levels are too low, it can lead to fatigue, low blood sugar, and weight gain.

Chronic stress is one of the most common causes of cortisol imbalances. To balance cortisol levels, it is important to reduce stress and practice relaxation techniques such as meditation and yoga. Adequate sleep, regular exercise, and a healthy diet can also help balance cortisol levels. In some cases, supplementation with adaptogenic herbs or medication may be necessary to support healthy cortisol levels.

Hormonal balance plays a crucial role in achieving optimal menstrual health. Each hormone in our body acts like a unique instrument in an orchestra, playing a vital role in the beautiful symphony of our bodies. The key hormones that play a significant role in menstrual health include estrogen, progesterone, testosterone, follicle-stimulating hormone (FSH), luteinizing hormone (LH), prolactin, thyroid hormones, and cortisol. Understanding the functions of each hormone, the effects of imbalances, and practical ways to achieve hormonal balance through a holistic approach is essential for taking control of your menstrual health and improving your overall well-being. By incorporating a balanced diet, regular exercise, stress management, and natural supplements, we can support our bodies and achieve a more balanced and harmonious hormonal symphony.

Chapter 3

Empowering Your Cycle: Fitness for Every Phase

We're going to talk about how to empower your menstrual cycle with fitness. Yep, you read that right! Exercise doesn't have to be a painful chore that you dread every month. In fact, you can tailor your workouts to work with your menstrual cycle, not against it. By understanding the different phases of your cycle and how they affect your body, you can optimize your fitness routine and get the most out of every workout.

Let's start with the follicular phase. During this phase, your body is preparing for ovulation, and your energy levels are high. This is the perfect time to focus on cardio and endurance training. Think of your body like a car and your energy levels like a gas tank. During the follicular phase, your gas tank is full, so you can push yourself to go further and longer. You'll also want to incorporate strength training to build lean muscle mass, which will help increase your metabolism and burn more calories throughout the day.

Next up is the ovulatory phase, also known as the "sweet spot" of your cycle. During this phase, your estrogen levels are at their peak, which means you have an extra burst of energy and your body is more receptive to building muscle. This is the time to push yourself with high-intensity interval training (HIIT) and plyometrics. These types of workouts will help you build strength and power, and you'll see quick improvements in your endurance and overall fitness level.

The luteal phase. This phase is all about self-care and recovery. Your body is preparing for menstruation, and your hormone levels are fluctuating. This can cause mood swings, fatigue, and muscle soreness. Instead of pushing yourself too hard, focus on low-impact exercises like yoga, Pilates, or swimming. These activities will help you stay active without putting too much strain on your body. You can also incorporate foam rolling and stretching to help alleviate muscle soreness and tension.

The menstrual phase. This is the time to slow down and listen to your body. You may experience cramps, fatigue, and bloating, so it's important to take it easy and focus on restorative exercises. This can include gentle yoga, walking, or even just stretching. By staying active during this phase, you can help alleviate cramps and boost your mood, but don't push yourself too hard. Remember, your body is going through a lot during your period, so it's important to be kind to yourself and prioritize rest and relaxation.

Your menstrual cycle doesn't have to be a hindrance to your fitness goals. By understanding the different phases and tailoring your workouts to work with your body, you can optimize your fitness routine and achieve your goals faster. So, get out there and empower your cycle with fitness!

Follicular Phase: "Revving Up"

I always tell my clients that the follicular phase is a great time to focus on cardio and endurance training. During this phase, your body is gearing up for ovulation, and your energy levels are high, like a full gas tank in a car. Just like a car with a full gas tank can go further and longer, your body is capable of more during this phase.

So, don't be afraid to push yourself during workouts and try out new challenges. You'll be amazed at how much progress you can make in just a few weeks. In addition to cardio, I highly recommend incorporating strength training into your routine during the follicular phase. By building lean muscle mass, you'll not only tone your body but also increase your metabolism.

Remember, everyone's body is different, so it's essential to listen to your body and adjust your workouts accordingly. Don't overdo it, and make sure to give yourself adequate rest and recovery time.

Phase-Specific Workouts

1. Light Resistance Training: Squats, Lunges, Bicep Curls, Shoulder Presses, Tricep Extensions
2. Cardio Training: Low-Intensity Steady State Cardio, Interval Training
3. Core and Balance Work: Planks, Pilates, Balance Workouts, Power Yoga
4. High-Intensity Interval Training: Burpees, Jump Squats, Mountain Climbers, Jumping Jacks
5. Flexibility Training: Stretching, Foam Rolling, Mobility Exercises

Ovulatory Phase: "Unleashing Your Power"

As we move into the ovulatory phase, things are really heating up! It's like your body is saying, "Let's do this!" Estrogen is running through your veins, giving you a burst of energy that makes you feel like you can conquer the world. You have an opportunity to make significant fitness gains during this phase, so it's important to take advantage of it.

To really make the most of this phase, I like to turn up the intensity with high - intensity interval training (HIIT) and plyometrics. These types of workouts really challenge your body and help you build strength and power. Think of it like a power surge you're tapping into all that extra energy and using it to push yourself harder than ever before.

With HIIT, you can really maximize your workout in a short amount of time. By combining high-intensity bursts of exercise with short rest periods, you'll get your heart rate up and burn more calories than you would with steady-state cardio. And the best part is, you'll continue to burn calories even after your workout is over thanks to the afterburn effect.

Plyometrics, on the other hand, focuses on explosive movements that work your muscles in a different way than traditional strength training. Think jumping jacks, box jumps, and burpees. These exercises require a lot of power and coordination, but they can be incredibly effective in building strength and increasing your overall fitness level.

So, during your ovulatory phase, it's time to push yourself and take your fitness to the next level. Incorporate HIIT and plyometrics into your workouts, and you'll see quick improvements in your endurance, strength, and overall fitness. Remember, your body is ready and willing to work hard during this phase, so don't be afraid to challenge yourself and go for it!

Phase-Specific Workouts

1. Core Workouts: Plank, Leg Raises, Crunches, Russian Twists
2. Cardio Workouts: Walking, Swimming, Cycling, Jumping Jacks
3. Strength Training: Squats, Lunges, Push-Ups, Weight Lifting
4. Flexibility Training: Yoga, Pilates, Stretching Exercises
5. Balance Training: Single-Leg Stance Exercises, Tai Chi
6. HIIT (High-Intensity Interval Training): Burpees, Jump Squats, Mountain Climbers

Luteal Phase: "Finding Balance"

As we move into the luteal phase, it's time to slow things down and focus on self-care. This is the time when your body is preparing for menstruation, and your hormones are all over the place. You might feel more emotional than usual, experience fatigue, or even have muscle soreness. So instead of pushing yourself too hard with high-intensity workouts, it's important to focus on low-impact exercises that help you stay active without adding extra strain to your body. Think of it as a time to recharge and rejuvenate yourself.

One of the best low-impact exercises to consider during the luteal phase is yoga. This practice is perfect for calming your mind and reducing stress, which is crucial during this phase. You can find a lot of yoga poses that help with menstrual cramps and bloating. The poses that focus on stretching the hips and lower back, like pigeon pose or child's pose, are especially helpful. Even if you're not into yoga, Pilates and swimming are great low-impact alternatives that still allow you to stay active and take care of your body.

Another way to help your body recover during the luteal phase is to incorporate foam rolling and stretching into your routine. Foam rolling is like giving your muscles a massage, which can help alleviate soreness and tension. Stretching, on the other hand, helps improve flexibility, mobility drills and CAR's can improve your joint health. These simple practices can make a huge difference in how you feel, especially during the luteal phase.

Phase-Specific Workouts/Selfcare

1. Core strengthening exercises: Reformer Pilates, pelvic floor activation
2. Low-impact cardio: Walking, swimming, cycling
3. Strength training exercises: Squats, lunges, push-ups
4. Yoga poses such as Child's Pose and Cat/Cow
5. Stretching and foam-rolling to reduce tension
6. Mindful breathing
7. Meditation and self-reflection
8. Gentle activities such as gardening or painting
9. Pre-menstrual self-care activities like taking a bath or massage

Menstrual Phase: "Honoring Your Body"

As someone who's been through her fair share of menstrual cycles, I know just how tough the menstrual phase can be. It's the time when your body is shedding its lining, and it can bring about a whole host of uncomfortable symptoms. From cramps to bloating to fatigue, it's essential to listen to your body and take things slow. This is the phase where you should prioritize restorative exercises like gentle yoga or stretching, which can help ease your cramps and alleviate your symptoms. Even just going for a walk can help boost your mood and give you a much-needed break from the demands of daily life.

But, as with all things related to your menstrual cycle, it's important not to push yourself too hard. Your body is already doing a lot of work during this phase, and over - exerting yourself can do more harm than good. You don't need to be running marathons or doing high-intensity workouts during this time. Instead, focus on giving your body the rest and relaxation it needs to recover and recharge.

One way to approach exercise during the menstrual phase is to think of it as a time for gentle, nourishing movement. Imagine your body as a plant that needs watering and nurturing to grow. By taking care of yourself in this way, you're helping to nourish and support your body during a time when it needs it most. It's all about finding the right balance between staying active, taking things slow, and listening to your body's cues.

Ultimately, the menstrual phase is a reminder that our bodies are incredible, complex systems that need our care and attention. By slowing down and taking the time to rest and restore, we can help support our bodies through the ups and downs of our menstrual cycles. So, don't be afraid to take it easy during this phase, and remember to prioritize self-care and self-love. Your body will thank you for it!

Phase-Specific Workouts/Selfcare

1. Slow and gentle yoga: Spend time doing slow, gentle yoga stretches that focus on relaxation and ease of movement.
2. Self-massage: Use warm oils and light pressure to massage your body, focusing on areas of tension and relaxation.
3. Meditation: Practice a simple meditation to help quiet your mind and relax your body.
4. Guided visualization: Take a few minutes to close your eyes and imagine a peaceful place, allowing yourself to relax and let go of any worries.
5. Breathing exercises: Use mindful breathing techniques to help your body relax and stay present in the moment.
6. Journaling: Spend some time writing down your thoughts and feelings. This can help you identify and process any emotions that may be causing stress or tension.
7. Hot bath or shower: Take a hot bath or shower to help your body relax and relieve any physical tension.
8. Eat healthy: Fuel your body with nutritious foods that can help you stay energized and relaxed.
9. Get plenty of rest. Make sure you're getting enough sleep during this time to help your body recharge and recover.
10. Spend time in nature. Take a walk in a park.

As someone who has struggled with menstrual cycle-related fatigue and cramps, I can tell you that following a cycle-based fitness routine can be life-changing. Not only does it help alleviate symptoms, but it also empowers you to feel more in tune with your body.

By listening to your body's natural rhythms, you can optimize your workouts and achieve better results. During the follicular phase, you'll have the energy to push yourself further and build lean muscle mass. During the ovulatory phase, you'll see quick improvements in your endurance and overall fitness level. During the luteal phase, you'll focus on recovery and self-care, which will help prevent injuries and burnout. And during the menstrual phase, you'll prioritize rest and relaxation, which will help you feel rejuvenated and ready to tackle your next workout.

But the benefits of cycle-based fitness go beyond physical improvements. By honoring your body's natural rhythms, you'll also feel more connected to your femininity and empowered as a woman. You'll learn to listen to your body's needs and prioritize self-care, which can have a positive impact on your overall well-being.

So, if you're tired of feeling like your menstrual cycle is holding you back from your fitness goals, it's time to try cycle-based fitness. Trust me, your body (and mind) will thank you!

Cycle based workout Plan

For all Body Types

		CARDIO	STRENGTH	YOGA
MENSTRUAL	Purify & begin Anew	Gardening Slow Walk Swimming	Pilates Resistance band training Mobility moves	Child's Pose Butterfly Puppy Pose
OVULATORY	Ignight Passion & Vitalize	Running Hiking HIIT	Weight Training (Core & Glutes) Functional Moves Swimming	Warrior Pelvic Bridge Shoulder stand & plough
LUTEAL	Rest & Restore	Pilates Cycling Long Walks	Resistance training (Thigh) Functional Core Static Holds	Pigeon Pose Forward Bends Goddess
FOLLICULAR	Nourish & create	Sprints Agility jump training Endurance Run, cycle or swim	Push & Pull training Deadlifts Full body Resistance	Headstand Crow & Peacock Triangle

Chapter 4

Nourishing Balance: Diet Tips for the Cycle phases

I know that our diet plays a significant role in balancing our hormones and maintaining overall health. I'll share some simple yet effective tips and tricks to help you stay healthy and nourished during each phase of your menstrual cycle.

The follicular phase is a time of new beginnings and fresh starts. It's the perfect time to add more greens and fresh fruits to your diet. These foods are high in antioxidants, which help protect our cells from damage. You can add some spinach to your smoothies or lentils to salads, or snack on some berries or an apple throughout the day. It's also essential to focus on healthy fats during this phase, which help support hormone production. Foods like nuts, seeds, and avocados are great sources of healthy fats and can easily be added to your meals.

As we move into the ovulatory phase, it's essential to focus on foods that support our energy levels and promote blood flow. Dark leafy greens, beets, and pomegranates are all great options. These foods are high in iron, which helps transport oxygen throughout the body and improve energy levels. It's also a great time to indulge in some healthy, plant-based sources of protein like lentils, chickpeas, and tofu. These foods can help keep you feeling full and satisfied throughout the day.

The luteal phase is a time when many of us experience mood swings, cramps, and bloating. To combat these symptoms, it's essential to focus on foods that reduce inflammation and support healthy digestion. Ginger, turmeric, and chamomile tea are all great options. You can also add some fermented foods like pickle or fermented rice kanji to your meals to support healthy gut bacteria. It's also important to focus on complex carbohydrates during this phase, which help to stabilize blood sugar levels and reduce cravings. Whole grains like rice, millets, and whole wheat bread are all excellent sources of complex carbs.

During the menstrual phase, it's time to focus on nourishing, easy-to-digest foods. Foods that are rich in iron and vitamin B12 can help replenish lost nutrients during this time. Spinach, beet greens, and lentils are all excellent sources of iron. Foods like tofu, plant-based milks, and nuts are great sources of vitamin B12. It's also important to focus on hydrating foods like watermelon and cucumber, which can help reduce bloating and improve digestion.

Following a balanced, vegetarian diet can help support a healthy menstrual cycle and overall well-being. By focusing on nutrient-dense foods during each phase of your cycle, you can nourish your body and reduce symptoms like mood swings, cramps, and bloating. Remember, small changes in your diet can have a significant impact on your health and well-being, so start by making small changes that work for you and your lifestyle.

Optimizing Intake During the Follicular Phase

Picture this: It's a beautiful spring day, and the trees are just starting to bud. The follicular phase is just like this a time of new beginnings and fresh starts. During this phase, our body is preparing for ovulation, and it's the perfect time to focus on adding more greens and fresh fruits to our diet.

Think of these foods as your own personal army, protecting your cells from damage like a superhero. Spinach and moringa (Drumstick leaves) are the stars of this army, with their high antioxidant content. You can easily add them to your smoothies or salads, or even create your own green smoothie bowl. If you're not a fan of greens, no worries; just add some berries or a seasonal fruit to your daily snacks. These fruits are also high in antioxidants and can be a sweet and delicious treat.

Healthy fats are also essential during the follicular phase, as they help support hormone production. Think of healthy fats as a secret weapon, a silent hero helping our body behind the scenes. Nuts, seeds, and avocados are amazing sources of healthy fats and can easily be added to your meals. You can sprinkle some chia seeds on your morning fruit bowl or top your salad with some walnuts or almonds. And let's not forget about avocados; you can add them to your toast or even make some guacamole for a snack.

Our Recommendations

1. Protein: aim for 25-30g of protein per meal. Good sources of vegetarian protein include beans, nuts, seeds, tofu, tempeh, yogurt, dairy, and quinoa.

2. Fats: aim for 15-20g of fat per meal. Good sources of vegetarian fats include avocado, olives, nuts, and nut butters.

3. Carbohydrates: aim for complex carbohydrates such as whole grains and starchy vegetables. Try to include a variety of fruits, vegetables, and legumes.

4. Fiber: aim for 25-35g of fiber per day. Good sources of fiber include fruits, vegetables, legumes, nuts, and seeds.
5. Vitamins and Minerals: aim to include a variety of fruits and vegetables to ensure adequate micronutrient intake.
6. Hydration: aim to drink at least 8 glasses of water per day.

Foods to include in this phase:

1. Dark leafy greens
   - Spinach (Palak): Spinach is a nutrient-dense dark green leafy vegetable that is rich in iron, folate, and vitamin K. It helps in reduce inflammation and improve digestion.
   - Mustard greens (Sarson ka saag): Mustard greens are a rich source of vitamins A, C, and K. It helps in improve bone health and reduce inflammation.
   - Amaranth leaves (Chaulai): Amaranth leaves are a rich source of calcium, iron, and vitamin A. It helps in improve digestion and regulate blood sugar levels.
   - Drumstick leaves (Moringa): Drumstick leaves are rich in antioxidants, vitamin C, and iron. It helps in reduce inflammation and improve gut health.
2. Legumes such as beans, lentils, and chickpeas
3. Healthy fats such as avocados, nuts, and seeds
4. Fruits and vegetables: Seasonal
5. Herbs
   - Shatavari: It is an adaptogenic herb that helps balance hormones and boost fertility.

- Ashwagandha: It helps to reduce stress and anxiety, which in turn can improve hormonal balance.
- Dong Quai: It has been used for centuries to support menstrual and reproductive health and to reduce menstrual cramps.
- Triphala: It helps to regulate the digestive system, which can have a positive effect on overall health and hormonal balance.

Effects of Nutritional Inadequacy

Inadequate intake during the Follicular Phase of your menstrual cycle can have a number of negative implications for your health. Not consuming enough essential nutrients such as iron, zinc, or vitamins can lead to fatigue, poor concentration, and even a weakened immune system. Similarly, consuming too many calories and unhealthy fats can lead to weight gain, an increased risk of chronic diseases, and hormonal imbalances. Taking the time to ensure that you are fueling your body with the right amount of nutrients during this phase is essential in order to maintain your health and wellbeing.

Eating for Hormonal Balance During the Ovulatory Phase

As we move into the ovulatory phase, think of your body as a car that needs a refill of petrol to keep it going. During this phase, our bodies are working hard to produce an egg and prepare for possible fertilization. That means we need to fuel our bodies with foods that will support our energy levels and promote blood flow.

Dark leafy greens, such as Gongura, are like a superhero cape for your body. They are high in iron, which is essential for transporting oxygen throughout the body and improving energy levels. Think of it as an energizing shot for your body that will keep you feeling strong and ready to take on the world.

Beets and pomegranates are also excellent choices during this phase. Think of them like a power bank for your body. They are packed with antioxidants, vitamins, and minerals that help keep your blood flowing and your energy levels high. They are also known to support healthy skin and a healthy heart.

It's also a great time to add in some healthy sources of protein like lentils, chickpeas, and tofu. Think of them like building blocks for your body. These plant-based proteins can help keep you feeling full and satisfied throughout the day while also supporting muscle growth and repair.

So let's get excited about nourishing our bodies and embracing our menstrual cycle with open arms.

Our Recommendations

1. Protein: Nuts, seeds, urad dal porridge
2. Healthy Fats: Desi ghee, coconut oil, butter, and nuts
3. Fibre: Whole grains, fruits, and vegetables
4. Magnesium: Leafy green vegetables, nuts, and seeds
5. Zinc, pumpkin seeds, and dark chocolate
6. Iron: leafy greens, dates
7. B Vitamins: Whole grains, legumes, and nuts
8. Vitamin E: Almonds, sunflower seeds

9. Vitamin D: Eggs, almond and soy milk
10. Omega-3 Fatty Acids: Chia seeds, and flaxseeds

Foods to include in this phase

1. Dark leafy greens
   - Curry leaves: Curry leaves are rich in antioxidants and help in improve digestion, reduce stress, and regulating hormones.
   - Drumstick leaves: Drumstick leaves are a great source of iron, calcium, and vitamin C, which help boost immunity and improve bone health.
   - Red sorrel leaves: Red sorrel leaves, also called as gongura, are rich in antioxidants and help promote healthy digestion and reduce menstrual cramps.
2. Nuts and seeds such as almonds, walnuts, and flaxseeds
3. Whole grains
4. Healthy fats such as avocado, olive oil, and coconut oil
5. Citrus fruits and berries
6. Herbs and spices
   - Holy Basil: It is an adaptogenic herb that can help reduce stress and improve hormonal balance.
   - Licorice Root: It helps to regulate hormonal levels and reduce inflammation.
   - Red Raspberry Leaf: It is a rich source of vitamins and minerals that support hormonal balance and reproductive health.

- Nettle Leaf: It helps to reduce inflammation and support overall hormonal health.

Effects of Nutritional Inadequacy

Having an inadequate intake during the ovulation phase of your menstrual cycle can be detrimental to your health. It can lead to a decrease in fertility, as your body is not receiving the nutrients it needs to support a healthy egg. It can also affect your hormone levels, leading to mood swings and other symptoms associated with PMS. In addition, it can lead to an imbalance in your reproductive system, leading to irregular menstrual cycles and other issues.

To ensure that you are getting the proper nutrition during your ovulation phase, it is important to focus on eating a balanced diet. This includes eating plenty of fruits and vegetables, as well as healthy fats. Additionally, you should make sure to get adequate amounts of vitamins and minerals.

Practicing Mindful Eating to Support Hormonal Balance During the Luteal Phase

One phase that can be particularly challenging is the luteal phase. You know, that time when you feel like you're about to snap at anyone who looks at you the wrong way? Yep, we've all been there. But don't worry, there are some simple things you can do to alleviate these symptoms and feel more like yourself again.

First up, let's talk about inflammation. It's like when you accidentally hit your funny bone and it swells up and hurts like crazy. Inflammation can happen in our bodies too, and it can cause all sorts of problems. But don't worry, there are some foods you can eat that can help reduce inflammation and make you feel better. Ginger, turmeric, and chamomile tea are like the superheroes of the food world when it comes to reducing inflammation. They can help soothe your body and make you feel more comfortable.

Next, let's talk about your gut. It's important to keep your gut healthy and happy during the luteal phase, and one way to do that is by eating fermented foods like kimchi or pickles. Think of these foods as little helpers that work inside your gut to keep everything running smoothly.

And lastly, let's talk about carbs. Yes, carbs! They're not the enemy, I promise. Complex carbs, like whole grains, can actually be really good for you during the luteal phase. They can help stabilize your blood sugar levels and reduce those pesky cravings that always seem to pop up at the worst times. So, think of whole grains like rice, millets, and whole wheat as your trusty sidekicks during this time.

Our Recommendations

1. Iron-rich foods such as legumes, dark leafy greens, nuts, and seeds

2. Calcium-rich foods such as plant milks, tofu, almonds, and sesame seeds

3. Magnesium-rich foods such as dark leafy greens, nuts and seeds, legumes, and whole grains

4. Zinc-rich foods such as legumes, nuts and seeds, and tempeh
7. Vitamin D-rich foods such as plant milks, mushrooms, and eggs
8. Omega-3 fatty acids found in flaxseeds, chia seeds, and walnuts

Are you struggling to manage your appetite during the luteal phase of your period cycle? Let me tell you why!

Women experience an increase in progesterone levels, which can affect their energy levels and metabolism. This hormonal shift often leads to an increase in appetite and the need for more calories. Providing your body with adequate nutrition during this phase is crucial to support its increased demands. The extra calories are necessary to fuel your body's activities, maintain hormonal balance, and support the intricate processes involved in preparing the uterus for a potential pregnancy. Additionally, consuming nutrient-dense foods during this phase can help alleviate common symptoms like mood swings, fatigue, and cravings. By honoring your body's need for additional calories during the luteal phase, you are prioritizing your overall well-being and supporting your body's natural rhythms.

How to practice mindful eating during the luteal phase?

1. **Start with small portions**: Serving yourself smaller portions can help you slow down and pay attention to your body's cues of hunger and fullness.
2. **Create a ritual**: Whether it's drinking a cup of tea or lighting a candle, creating a ritual can help you focus on

the mindful eating process and tap into your body's hormones.

3. **Take mindful pauses**: Taking mindful pauses throughout your meal can help you check in with your body and be mindful of your hunger and fullness.

Foods to include in this phase

1. Dark leafy greens
    - Amaranth leaves: Also known as chaulai or lal saag, amaranth leaves are a good source of calcium, iron, and vitamins A and C. They help reduce inflammation and promote healthy digestion.
    - Fenugreek leaves: Fenugreek leaves, or methi, are rich in antioxidants, iron, and vitamins A and C. They help to regulate hormones and reduce the severity of cramps during the luteal phase.
    - Mustard greens: Mustard greens, or sarson ka saag, are a good source of vitamins A, C, and K, as well as folate and calcium. They help to reduce bloating, inflammation, and water retention.
2. Whole grains and millets
3. Legumes such as beans, lentils, and chickpeas
4. Fruits such as oranges, strawberries, and kiwis
5. Nuts and seeds such as almonds, walnuts, and flaxseeds
6. Herbs
    - Maca: It helps to regulate hormones and improve energy levels, mood, and libido.

- Rhodiola: It helps to reduce stress and improve energy levels, which can be beneficial during the luteal phase when many women experience PMS symptoms.

- Vitex: It helps to regulate the menstrual cycle and reduce PMS symptoms such as breast tenderness, bloating, and mood swings.

- Evening Primrose Oil: It contains gamma-linolenic acid (GLA), which can help reduce PMS symptoms such as breast tenderness and mood swings.

Maximizing Nutrient Density During Menstruation

When it comes to your own menstrual cycle, it's important to understand that each phase has its unique nutritional needs. During the menstrual phase, your body is working hard to shed its lining, which means you're losing important nutrients that need to be replenished. It's kind of like when you finish a tough workout and need to refuel with some nourishing foods.

So, what kind of foods should you be eating during this phase? Think of it like building a fortress to protect your body. You want to focus on foods that are rich in iron, which is like building a strong foundation. This nutrient helps replenish the blood you've lost during your period and prevent anemia. Nuts, spinach, and lentils are all excellent sources of iron, and they're also delicious and easy to incorporate into your meals.

You'll also want to focus on foods that are rich in vitamin B12, which is like adding strong walls to your fortress. This nutrient helps keep your nerves and blood cells healthy, and it's found in foods like tofu, and plant-based milks. These foods are great sources of energy and will help keep you feeling your best.

Finally, it's important to stay hydrated during this phase, which is like adding a moat around your fortress. Hydrating foods like watermelon, cucumber, and celery can help to reduce bloating and improve digestion. So, make sure to drink plenty of water and eat plenty of hydrating foods to keep your body feeling balanced and energized.

Our Recommendations

1. Calcium: Helps maintain strong bones and can reduce cramping. Sources include dairy, leafy greens
2. Magnesium: Necessary for healthy muscle and nerve function. Sources include whole grains, nuts, and legumes.
3. Vitamin D: Enhances calcium absorption and bone health. Sources include, sunlight exposure.
4. Iron: Aids in oxygen transport and energy production. Sources include lean meats, legumes.
5. Vitamin B6: Helps with the metabolism of carbohydrates, fats, and proteins sources
6. Vitamin B12: Aids in the production of red blood cells.
7. Folate: Necessary for the production of DNA and red blood cells. Sources include enriched grains, dark leafy greens, and legumes.
8. Zinc: Supports immune system function and wound healing. Sources include nuts, and seeds.

9. Omega-3 Fatty Acids: Reduce inflammation and improve mood

Effects of Nutritional Inadequacy

Having an adequate nutrient intake during the menstrual phase is essential for the maintenance of overall health and well-being. Nutrients such as iron, folate, and vitamins A, B, C, and E are especially important during this time as they can help reduce fatigue and assist the body in withstanding the physical and emotional demands of the period and Eating a balanced diet rich in fruits, vegetables, whole grains, healthy fats can help ensure that your body is getting the nutrients it needs to stay healthy.

Foods to include in this phase

1. Dark leafy greens
   - Beet greens (Chukandar ka saag): Beet greens are a rich source of vitamin C, iron, and antioxidants. It helps improve heart health and reduces menstrual cramps.
   - Coriander leaves (Dhaniya): Coriander leaves are a rich source of antioxidants, vitamin C, and minerals like calcium and iron. It helps improve digestion and reduces menstrual cramps.
   - Amaranth leaves: Amaranth leaves, also known as chaulai or lal saag, are another nutritious green that can be consumed during menstruation. They are high in iron, calcium, and vitamins A and C, which can help improve blood flow and reduce cramps. You can

use amaranth leaves in dishes like stir-fries, curries, or soups.

2. Iron-rich foods
3. Legumes such as beans, lentils, and chickpeas
4. Nuts and seeds such as almonds, walnuts, and flaxseeds
5. Fruits such as bananas, oranges, and strawberries
6. Herbs and spices
   - Ginger: It helps to relieve menstrual cramps, reduce inflammation, and improve circulation.
   - Fennel: It is known for its ability to relieve menstrual cramps, bloating, and other menstrual-related discomforts.
   - Cinnamon: It can help regulate menstrual cycles and reduce heavy bleeding.
   - Chamomile: It helps to reduce menstrual cramps, relieve anxiety, and promote relaxation.

Managing Cravings and Mood Swings

For women, managing cravings and mood swings during the period cycle can be a difficult task. To help manage these cravings and mood swings, it is important to understand the phases of the cycle. During the preovulatory phase, women experience an increase in energy and libido. This is the time to go easy on cravings, as they can be hard to resist. During the ovulatory phase, it is important to focus on healthy eating habits and exercise, as this will help to keep cravings under control and reduce mood swings.

The luteal phase of the period cycle is when hormones start to fluctuate and cravings can become more intense. To help manage these cravings, it is important to focus on healthy foods, and limit processed and sugary foods. Additionally, engaging in activities such as yoga, meditation, and journaling can help reduce mood swings and keep cravings in check. Finally, it is important to get enough sleep during this time, as this helps to regulate hormones and reduce cravings and mood swings.

Three strategies that can help you manage cravings and mood swings

1. **Exercise**: Exercise can help keep your moods and energy levels stable during the menstrual cycle phases. Exercise releases endorphins, which are natural hormones that can help boost feelings of happiness and reduce stress.

2. **Eat Balanced Meals**: Eating regular, balanced meals can help keep your blood sugar levels stable, which can help reduce cravings and mood swings. Try to include foods that are rich in complex carbohydrates and healthy fats.

3. **Get Enough Sleep**: Getting at least seven to eight hours of sleep each night can help reduce stress and improve your overall energy levels. Sleep deprivation can worsen mood swings and cravings, so it's important to get enough rest.

It is important to recognize that if cravings and mood swings are not managed during the menstrual cycle phases, they can have serious effects on both physical and mental health.

Women who do not take steps to manage their cravings and mood swings may find that their symptoms worsen, leading to irritability, depression, and other physical ailments. Furthermore, cravings and mood swings may increase the risk of unhealthy behaviors, like overeating.

Finally, research has shown that if cravings and mood swings are not properly managed, they can lead to longer, heavier, and more painful periods. Therefore, it is essential for women to take steps to manage their cravings and mood swings to ensure that their menstrual cycle phases are as comfortable and healthy as possible.

Utilizing Herbs and Other Natural Remedies to Support Balance

Herbs have been used for centuries in India to support balance and health. Traditional Indian herbs such as Ashoka, Shatavari, and Guduchi are especially beneficial for women's health, providing nourishment and strengthening the reproductive system. All of these herbs provide essential nutrients, vitamins, and minerals that can help reduce the effects of stress, regulate hormones, and strengthen the uterus. Furthermore, these herbs can help reduce bloating, cramps, fatigue, and mood swings associated with the menstrual cycle.

My Favorites

1. Ashwagandha: Used to improve the overall balance of the female reproductive hormones, reduce stress and anxiety, and prevent hair loss.
2. Shatavari: Enhances fertility, increases libido, and helps regulate the menstrual cycle.

3. Brahmi: Helps reduce stress and anxiety, improve cognitive function, and treat depression.
4. Guduchi: Used to reduce inflammation, improve immunity, and balance hormones.
5. Amla: Increases fertility and boosts energy levels.
6. Licorice: Used to reduce menstrual pain and cramps.
7. Turmeric: Helps reduce inflammation, improve digestion, and maintain hormonal balance.

Our Tea Blend Recommendations

Menstrual Phase:

1. Ginger and Turmeric Tea: Helps relieve menstrual cramps and reduce inflammation in the body.
2. Cinnamon and Fennel Tea: Aid in regulating menstrual flow and reducing bloating.
3. Chamomile and Lemon Balm Tea: Soothe the nervous system, helping to reduce anxiety and promote relaxation.
4. Raspberry Leaf and Nettle Tea: Helps tone the uterus and balance hormones, reducing heavy bleeding and menstrual pain.

Follicular Phase:

1. Licorice (Adhimaturam) and Ashwagandha Tea: Supports healthy ovulation and balances hormones.
2. Red Clover and Dandelion Tea: Helps to detoxify the liver and support the body's natural cleansing processes.

3. Cardamom and Rose Tea: Reduces stress and promotes a sense of calm.
4. Peppermint and Lemon Tea: Aid in digestion and reduce bloating.

Ovulatory Phase:

1. Shatavari and Maca Tea: Boosts fertility and supports healthy ovulation.
2. Hawthorn and Passionflower Tea: Helps reduce anxiety and promote relaxation.
3. Cinnamon and Fenugreek Tea: Aids in regulating menstrual flow and supports hormonal balance.
4. Chaste Tree (Nirgundi) and Red Raspberry Leaf Tea: Balances hormones and supports the reproductive system.

Luteal Phase:

1. Brahmi and Ashwagandha Tea: Supports a healthy stress response and reduces anxiety.
2. Ginger and Lemon Balm Tea: Helps reduce bloating and digestive discomfort.
3. Chamomile and Lavender Tea: Promotes relaxation and supports a healthy sleep cycle.
4. Skullcap and Passionflower Tea: Reduces anxiety and promotes a sense of calm.

Chapter 5

Menstrual Health and Sexual Wellness: Understanding the Connection and Enhancing Your Pleasure

As a woman, I have always been fascinated by the intricate connections between my menstrual cycle and my sexual wellness. The menstrual cycle is not just about shedding of the uterine lining; it is a complex interplay of hormones that impact our physical, emotional, and sexual health. Understanding this connection can help us enhance our sexual pleasure and empower us to take charge of our menstrual and sexual health.

We will delve into the ways in which our menstrual cycles impact our sexual drive and how we can work with our bodies to enhance our pleasure. From self-care during menstruation to exploring sexual wellness practices, we will learn how to embrace our bodies and celebrate our femininity.

Many women experience issues such as pain during sex, low libido, or difficulty achieving orgasm, which can be linked to hormonal fluctuations during the menstrual cycle. By understanding the root causes of these issues, we can seek appropriate treatment and work towards a more fulfilling sexual life.

Self-care during menstruation is crucial for enhancing our sexual wellness. We will explore a range of self-care practices, from nutrition to exercise, that can help us feel our best during our periods. Additionally, we will delve into the use of menstrual products, such as menstrual cups, tampons, and pads, and how they can impact our sexual experiences.

Let's celebrate our bodies, embrace our femininity, and enhance our pleasure.

The Hormonal Connection: How Menstrual Cycles Impact Sexual Desire

The hormonal changes that occur during the menstrual cycle can have a significant impact on a woman's sexual desire and overall sexual wellness. Understanding how these changes affect the body and mind is essential to promoting healthy and fulfilling sexual experiences throughout the month.

The menstrual cycle is a complex process that involves a delicate balance of hormones. Throughout the month, levels of estrogen, progesterone, and testosterone fluctuate, leading to different physical and emotional changes. During the first half of the cycle, estrogen levels rise, leading to an increase in energy, mood, and sexual desire. This is the time when many women report feeling the most sexually active.

However, as the menstrual cycle progresses, estrogen levels drop, and progesterone levels rise. This shift can lead to feelings of fatigue, mood swings, and a decrease in sexual desire. Additionally, many women experience physical symptoms such as bloating, breast tenderness, and cramps, which can further impact sexual wellness.

The hormonal changes that occur during the menstrual cycle can have a significant impact on sexual desire and overall sexual wellness. By understanding the relationship between menstrual health and sexual wellness, women can take steps to promote healthy and fulfilling sexual experiences throughout the month.

Self-Care During Menstruation: Enhancing Sexual Wellness

Taking care of ourselves during our menstrual cycle is crucial for our overall health and well-being. However, many women often forget that self-care can also enhance their sexual wellness. Let's explore the importance of self-care during menstruation and how it can positively impact our sexual pleasure.

Menstruation is a natural and necessary process, but it can also be physically and emotionally challenging. Common symptoms such as cramps, bloating, nausea, and fatigue can make it difficult to feel our best. Taking care of ourselves during this time is crucial, not only for our physical health but also for our mental health.

Self-care during menstruation can help alleviate symptoms and enhance our overall well-being. It can also positively impact our sexual wellness. When we feel good about ourselves, our bodies, and our mental state, we are more likely to enjoy and engage in sexual activity.

Self-Care Practices to Enhance Sexual Wellness During Menstruation

1. **Exercise:** Hip stretches and mobility can help alleviate menstrual cramps and boost endorphins, which can improve our mood and overall well-being. It can also increase blood flow to the pelvic area, which can enhance sexual pleasure.

2. **Nutrition:** Eating a healthy, balanced diet during menstruation can help reduce bloating and fatigue. Certain

foods, such as dark chocolate, can also boost mood and increase sexual desire.

3. **Rest:** Getting enough rest during menstruation is crucial for our physical and mental health. Lack of sleep can lead to fatigue and irritability, which can negatively impact sexual wellness.

4. **Self-Massage:** Massaging the abdomen and lower back can help alleviate menstrual cramps and promote relaxation. It can also increase blood flow to the pelvic area.

5. **Mindfulness:** Practicing mindfulness during menstruation can help reduce stress and anxiety, which can improve our overall well-being. Mindfulness techniques such as meditation and deep breathing can also enhance sexual pleasure by increasing our ability to focus and be present in the moment.

6. **Sexual Exploration:** Menstruation can be a time of increased sensitivity and arousal. Exploring our bodies through masturbation or sexual activity with a partner can enhance sexual pleasure and promote intimacy.

By incorporating self-care practices, we can enhance our sexual pleasure and promote intimacy with ourselves and our partners. Remember to prioritize self-care during menstruation and embrace this time as an opportunity for growth, exploration, and enhanced sexual wellness.

Menstruation and Sexual Dysfunction

Sexual dysfunction is a common problem that affects many women, and it can be even more challenging for those who also experience menstrual issues. Menstruation and sexual dysfunction often have a complicated relationship, as menstrual pain, hormonal changes, and other issues can all contribute to sexual problems. Fortunately, there are many holistic and mindful treatment options available.

Before we explore treatment options, it's important to understand the connection between menstruation and sexual dysfunction. Menstruation can contribute to sexual dysfunction in a number of ways. For example, menstrual pain can make sex uncomfortable, and hormonal changes can lead to a decrease in sexual desire. Additionally, certain menstrual disorders, such as endometriosis and polycystic ovary syndrome (PCOS), can contribute to sexual dysfunction.

When seeking help for menstrual and sexual dysfunction, it's important to consider a range of treatment options. While medical interventions such as hormonal therapy or surgery may be necessary in some cases, there are also many holistic and mindful approaches that can be effective.

1. **Mindfulness and Meditation:** Mindfulness practices such as meditation can be helpful in reducing stress and anxiety, which can contribute to sexual dysfunction. Mindfulness can also help you connect with your body and become more aware of your physical sensations.

2. **Yoga:** Yoga can be an effective tool for managing menstrual pain and improving sexual function. Certain

yoga poses can help alleviate menstrual pain and increase circulation to the pelvic region, which can enhance sexual pleasure.

3. **Acupuncture:** Acupuncture is an ancient Chinese medical practice that involves inserting thin needles into the skin to stimulate specific points on the body. Acupuncture can be helpful in managing menstrual pain and improving sexual function.

4. **Dietary Changes:** Certain foods can be helpful in managing menstrual and sexual issues. For example, foods that are high in antioxidants and anti-inflammatory compounds can help reduce menstrual pain.

5. **Herbal Remedies:** Certain herbs, such as Shatavari and Ashwagandha, have been used for centuries. Herbal remedies can be a gentle and effective way to manage symptoms.

6. **Therapy:** Therapy can be helpful in addressing the psychological factors that contribute to sexual dysfunction. A therapist can help you work through issues such as anxiety, depression, and relationship problems.

Menstrual and sexual dysfunction can be challenging issues to manage, but there are many holistic and mindful treatment options available. It's important to remember that there is no one-size-fits-all approach to treatment, and what works for one person may not work for another. It's important to work with a healthcare provider who can help you identify the best treatment options for your unique needs.

The connection between menstrual health and sexual wellness is complex and multifaceted, and there is much to learn and explore in this field. By prioritizing self-care during menstruation, addressing sexual dysfunction, and promoting empowerment and education, we can work towards a world where women are able to enjoy optimal health and wellness in all aspects of their lives.

Chapter 6

Fertility Awareness Method: Tracking Your Cycle for Birth Control and Pregnancy

Let's delve into the science of fertility and explore the various natural birth control alternatives available. As someone who is interested in learning more about fertility awareness, I believe that it is essential to understand the female reproductive system and how it functions.

The use of hormonal birth control pills is widespread, but it is essential to note that they come with potential side effects. With the rise of interest in natural and holistic approaches to health and wellness, more people are exploring alternatives to hormonal birth control. The Fertility Awareness Method (FAM) is one such alternative that involves tracking your menstrual cycle to identify the fertile window and make informed decisions about birth control or trying to conceive.

To understand FAM, we must first understand the female reproductive system. The Science of Fertility will explain the complex processes involved in ovulation, fertilization, and implantation. We will also examine the different hormones that regulate the menstrual cycle and the various factors that can affect the timing and regularity of menstruation.

Beyond the Pill, we will look at the natural birth control alternatives available to individuals who prefer not to use hormonal birth control. We will explore the pros and cons of each method, including FAM, and discuss how they work to prevent pregnancy.

The Art of Observation is needed to focus on the techniques used in FAM, such as tracking basal body temperature and cervical mucus. We will delve into the science behind these techniques and how they can be used to identify the fertile window accurately.

Finally, we will discuss a holistic approach to fertility awareness, combining nutrition and lifestyle changes with FAM. We will explore the impact of diet, exercise, stress, and sleep on the menstrual cycle and how making positive changes in these areas can improve overall reproductive health.

I will provide you with a comprehensive overview of the Fertility Awareness Method and the various natural birth control alternatives available. By the end of this chapter, you will have a greater understanding of your body's natural rhythms and how to use this knowledge to make informed decisions about your reproductive health.

The Science of Fertility: Understanding the Female Reproductive System

As a woman who has been using the Fertility Awareness Method (FAM) for several years now, I believe that understanding the science behind the female reproductive system is crucial for successfully using this method for birth control or pregnancy achievement.

The female reproductive system is complex, but once you understand the basic anatomy and physiology, it becomes easier to track your cycle and identify your fertile and infertile days. The reproductive system consists of the ovaries, fallopian tubes, uterus, cervix, and vagina. These organs work together to create and transport the egg, prepare the uterus for implantation, and provide an environment for the growing fetus.

The menstrual cycle is the result of a complex interplay of hormones, which are produced by the hypothalamus, pituitary gland, and ovaries. These hormones regulate the growth and maturation of the egg, the thickening of the uterine lining, and the shedding of the lining if conception does not occur. The cycle begins on the first day of menstruation and typically lasts around 28 days, although it can be shorter or longer for some women.

There are several key events that occur during the menstrual cycle that are important for fertility awareness. The first is ovulation, which is the release of a mature egg from the ovary. Ovulation typically occurs around day 14 of the cycle but can vary depending on the length of your cycle. The second event is the production of cervical mucus, which is a fluid that is secreted by the cervix in response to hormones. The quantity and quality of cervical mucus change throughout the cycle, becoming more abundant and stretchy around the time of ovulation.

By tracking your menstrual cycle and observing changes in cervical mucus and basal body temperature, you can identify your fertile and infertile days. This knowledge is invaluable for using FAM for birth control or pregnancy achievement. However, it is important to note that FAM is not foolproof and requires commitment and consistency to be effective.

Beyond the Pill: Exploring Natural Birth Control Alternatives

As someone who has tried different forms of birth control over the years, I know how daunting it can be to choose the right method. For many women, the pill is often the first option presented by doctors, but it's important to know that there are natural alternatives available.

When I first learned about FAM, I was skeptical. The idea of tracking my cycle and relying on it for birth control seemed like a lot of work. However, after doing more research and talking to others who were using the method, I became intrigued. I learned that FAM involves tracking your menstrual cycle to determine when you are fertile and then avoiding intercourse or using other forms of protection during that time. This is done by monitoring your cervical mucus, basal body temperature, and other fertility signs.

What I love about FAM is that it's a completely natural and hormone-free method of birth control. Unlike the pill, which can have negative side effects and disrupt natural hormonal cycles, FAM works with your body's natural rhythms. It's also empowering to know exactly what's happening in my body at any given time and to have control over my fertility.

Of course, FAM is not foolproof, and it does require dedication and consistency. It's important to track your cycle consistently and to have open communication with your partner about your fertility and birth control needs. However, I've found that the benefits far outweigh the challenges.

There are other natural birth control methods available as well, such as barrier methods like condoms and diaphragms. It's important to do your research and talk to a healthcare provider to find the method that works best for you.

If you're looking for a natural and hormone-free alternative to traditional birth control methods, I highly recommend exploring the Fertility Awareness Method. It may take some time to get used to, but the benefits are worth it. Plus, you'll gain a greater understanding and appreciation for your body's natural rhythms and cycles.

The Art of Observation: Understanding Basal Body Temperature and Cervical Mucus

Two key indicators of fertility are basal body temperature (BBT) and cervical mucus, both of which can provide valuable insight into the state of your reproductive health.

BBT is your body's temperature at rest, and it can vary throughout your menstrual cycle due to fluctuations in hormone levels. By taking your temperature first thing in the morning before you get out of bed, you can track your BBT over time and identify patterns that indicate ovulation. Typically, BBT rises slightly after ovulation due to an increase in progesterone levels, which can help you pinpoint your fertile window.

Cervical mucus is another key indicator of fertility, as it changes in consistency and amount throughout your menstrual cycle. During the first part of your cycle, cervical mucus is typically thick and sticky, which makes it difficult for sperm to penetrate. As you approach ovulation, however, your cervical mucus becomes thinner and more stretchy, resembling raw egg whites. This fertile cervical mucus helps sperm travel more easily through the cervix and into the uterus, increasing your chances of conception.

By observing changes in your BBT and cervical mucus over time, you can become more attuned to your body's natural rhythms and use this knowledge to either prevent or promote pregnancy. For example, if you're trying to avoid pregnancy, you can abstain from sex or use barrier methods during your fertile window (when your BBT is elevated and your cervical mucus is thin and stretchy). On the other hand, if you're trying to conceive, you can have sex during your fertile window to increase your chances of success.

It's worth noting that tracking your BBT and cervical mucus can take some practice, and it's important to be consistent and accurate in your observations. You can use a BBT thermometer to take your temperature each morning, and you can check your cervical mucus by wiping with toilet paper or inserting a clean finger into your vagina. By keeping a record of your observations in a chart or app, you can track your progress over time and identify patterns that can help you make informed decisions about your reproductive health.

The art of observation is a powerful tool for understanding your body's natural rhythms and using that knowledge to make informed decisions about birth control and pregnancy.

A Holistic Approach: Combining Fertility Awareness with Nutrition and Lifestyle Changes.

I've learned that tracking your cycle is just one piece of the puzzle. Taking a holistic approach that incorporates nutrition and lifestyle changes can help support reproductive health and optimize your chances of conceiving. I'll share my tips and insights for combining FAM with healthy habits that support your overall well-being.

Diet and Nutrition

Your diet plays a crucial role in supporting reproductive health. Eating a well-balanced, nutrient-dense diet can help regulate your menstrual cycle, support hormone balance, and improve your chances of conceiving. Here are some dietary tips to keep in mind:

1. Focus on whole, nutrient-dense foods: Eating a variety of fruits, vegetables, whole grains, and healthy fats can provide the vitamins and minerals your body needs to support reproductive health.
2. Pay attention to macronutrient balance: Consuming a balanced ratio of carbohydrates, proteins, and fats can help regulate hormones and support overall health.
3. Reduce processed foods and refined sugars: Eating a diet high in junk food and sugary drinks can disrupt hormone balance and negatively affect reproductive health.
4. Stay hydrated: Drinking plenty of water can help keep your cervical mucus healthy and support your overall reproductive health.

Sleep and Circadian Rhythm

Getting enough quality sleep and maintaining a regular sleep schedule can also support reproductive health. Here are some tips to help you get the sleep you need:

1. Aim for 7-8 hours of sleep per night: Getting enough sleep can help regulate hormone levels and support reproductive health.
2. Stick to a regular sleep schedule: Going to bed and waking up at the same time each day can help regulate your body's circadian rhythm.
3. Create a bedtime routine: Establishing a relaxing bedtime routine can help prepare your body for sleep and improve sleep quality.

Exercise and Physical Activity

Physical activity can also support reproductive health by reducing stress, promoting hormone balance, and improving overall health. Here are some tips to keep in mind:

1. Aim for regular physical activity: Regular exercise can help regulate hormone levels and support reproductive health. Find an activity you enjoy, such as walking, yoga, or cycling, and aim for at least 30 minutes of moderate activity most days of the week.
2. Avoid over-exercising: Excessive exercise can disrupt hormone balance and negatively affect reproductive health.

Stress Reduction

Stress can negatively affect reproductive health by disrupting hormone balance and menstrual cycles. Here are some tips to help reduce stress:

1. Practice stress-reducing techniques: Techniques such as deep breathing, meditation, and yoga can help reduce stress and support reproductive health.

2. Prioritize self-care: Taking time to care for yourself can help reduce stress and improve overall well-being. Make time for activities you enjoy, such as reading, spending time in nature, or taking a relaxing bath.

Incorporating healthy habits such as nutrition and lifestyle changes can help support reproductive health and optimize your chances of conceiving. By combining FAM with these holistic practices, you can take a proactive approach to your reproductive health and overall well-being.

Chapter 7

Rejuvenating For Renewal: Yoga for Post-Menstrual Recovery

I want to talk about the importance of post-menstrual recovery and how yoga can help us rejuvenate for renewal. We'll dive into the benefits of yoga for menstrual health and explore a yoga sequence designed specifically for post-menstrual recovery.

So, why is post-menstrual recovery so important? Just like any physical activity, our menstrual cycle requires energy and resources from our body. During our period, our body goes through a lot of changes and stress, which can lead to fatigue and depletion. The postmenstrual phase is the perfect time to replenish our energy and restore balance to our body. Yoga is a fantastic way to achieve this balance and support our menstrual health.

In addition to the physical benefits of yoga, practicing yoga also supports our mental and emotional well-being. Yoga can help us manage stress, reduce anxiety, and improve our overall mood. This is particularly important during the post-menstrual phase when we may experience hormonal fluctuations and emotional sensitivity. Taking some time to practice yoga and focus on our breath can help us feel more centered and grounded.

Practicing yoga during the postmenstrual phase can be a powerful tool for rejuvenation and renewal. It can help us replenish our energy, restore balance to our bodies and support our mental and emotional well-being. So, next time you're feeling depleted after your period, give yoga a try and see how it can benefit your menstrual health. Remember to listen to your body and modify the poses as needed to ensure a safe and comfortable practice. Om!

Child's Pose

Child's pose is an effective yoga pose that can provide a variety of benefits to women. To do the pose, begin on your hands and knees, sit back on your heels, and stretch your arms out in front of you. To deepen the pose, you can lower your chest to the floor. When done correctly, child's pose helps to stretch and relax the muscles in the back, shoulders, and hips while also calming the mind. It also helps to relieve tension, fatigue, and stress, making it an ideal pose for women who are feeling overwhelmed. In addition, it can help improve posture, digestion, and breathing.

To get into the pose

1. Begin by kneeling on the floor with your toes together and your knees hip-width apart.
2. Bring your big toes together and spread your knees wide so that your buttocks can rest on your heels.
3. Take a deep breath and bring your arms down to your sides, palms facing up.
4. As you exhale, slowly bring your torso down so that your chest is resting on your thighs and your forehead is touching the floor.
5. Make sure your arms are extended alongside your body with your palms pressed against the floor.
6. Hold the pose for up to a minute, breathing deeply.

7. When you're ready to come out of the pose, slowly bring yourself up to a seated position and take a few moments to relax and enjoy the benefits of child's pose.

Downward Facing Dog

Downward Facing Dog is an incredibly beneficial yoga pose for women. It helps to improve posture and flexibility. It strengthens the arms, legs, and back while also stretching the shoulders, hamstrings, and calves. It also improves core strength, which is important for stability and balance. Additionally, it helps to reduce stress, anxiety, and fatigue and can even help to improve circulation and digestion.

To get into the pose

1. Begin by coming onto your hands and knees.

2. Place your hands shoulder-width apart and spread your fingers wide.

3. Tuck your toes under and press your hips up into the air, creating an inverted 'V' shape with your body.

4. Engage your core, tucking your pelvis out and push your tail bone towards the sky. Keep your legs slightly bent and your heels reaching for the floor.

5. Relax your head and neck, and breathe deeply. Hold for five to ten breaths, then release and come back to your hands and knees.

6. Enjoy the feeling of openness and strength that Downward Facing Dog brings.

Bridge Pose

Bridge Pose helps stretch your hips and chest, as well as opening your heart and lungs. Its main purpose is to help open the chest and increase flexibility in the shoulders, chest, and neck. By opening the chest and shoulders, Bridge pose can help increase the range of motion in your upper body, and strengthen the spine and abdominal muscles, providing further support for the back. This pose can also help improve your posture and alleviate tightness in the neck and shoulders.

To get into the pose

1. Being lying down on your back with feet on the floor

2. Raise your hips to the sky and ensure your knees are directly over your ankles.

3. Press your hands into the ground as you draw your shoulder blades together and widen your chest.

4. Lower the hip and slowly return back to the floor.

Forward Fold

The Forward Fold is a great way to cool your system down, as it helps to stretch your hamstrings and back. The forward fold yoga pose is an easy and effective way to relax and relieve tension in the body. This pose helps to increase flexibility, improve digestion, and reduce fatigue. It can also help to relax the mind and improve concentration. When practiced regularly, the forward fold yoga pose can help you feel more grounded and connected to your body.

To get into the pose

1. Start by standing with your feet hip width apart and your arms at your sides.

2. Take a deep breath and as you exhale, begin to hinge forward from your hips, keeping your back flat, and shift your body weight into your toes.

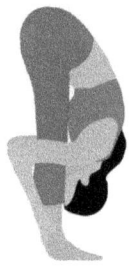

3. Allow your arms to hang down towards the floor, and let your head and neck relax.

4. Hold for several breaths, focusing on relaxing your body and letting your head hang heavy.

5. To come out of the pose, use your core muscles to slowly bring your torso back up to standing.

6. Take a few breaths here and then gently shake out your arms and legs before continuing with your practice.

The cobra

The cobra pose is a powerful yoga posture that can be used to promote post period cycle health in women. It is a gentle yet effective way to help restore balance to the body and mind while allowing for increased flexibility, strength, and energy.

To get into the pose

1. Start by lying flat on your stomach with your legs extended behind you.
2. Press your palms firmly into the mat, engaging your arm muscles. Keep your elbows close to your body.
3. Inhale deeply as you begin to lift your head, chest, and upper abdomen off the mat.
4. Continue lifting your torso, using the strength of your back muscles. Keep your shoulders relaxed and away from your ears. Focus on lengthening your spine and stretching forward through the crown of your head.
5. To release the pose, exhale and slowly lower your torso back down to the mat, vertebra by vertebra, until your forehead touches the floor. Relax your arms by your sides.

Rejuvenating and restoring balance after your period cycle is an essential aspect of maintaining overall menstrual health. It requires taking care of both the physical and emotional wellbeing of the body. Engaging in relaxation activities, eating a balanced diet, getting enough rest and exercise, and practicing yoga are some of the ways to achieve post-menstrual recovery. Yoga, in particular, is a powerful tool that can help stretch, relax, and renew the body.

I cannot stress enough the importance of taking care of oneself, especially after experiencing the physical and emotional changes during the menstrual cycle. By taking a holistic approach to renewal, you can achieve a sense of balance and peace, which can help you navigate your day-to-day life with more ease and grace. Incorporating yoga into your postmenstrual recovery journey can be a powerful tool to help you achieve that balance. With regular practice, you can cultivate a sense of inner strength, flexibility, and resilience, allowing you to face the challenges of life with a calm and centered mind. Remember to always listen to your body and honor its needs, so you can continue to nurture and support it throughout your menstrual cycle and beyond.

Chapter 8

Managing Pain and Discomfort: Natural Remedies for Menstrual Cramps

As women, we all know how uncomfortable menstrual cramps can be. For some of us, it's a minor inconvenience that lasts for a day or two. For others, it can be a debilitating experience that leaves us unable to carry out our daily activities. Regardless of the severity level, menstrual cramps can be frustrating and even discouraging, especially when we feel like we've tried everything to relieve the pain.

Let's explore a variety of natural remedies for menstrual cramps that can help alleviate discomfort and pain. We'll discuss the causes, symptoms, and severity levels of menstrual cramps and then dive into some mind-body techniques, dietary and nutritional strategies, heat therapy and hydrotherapy, aromatherapy and essential oils, topical applications, and massage therapy that can help manage menstrual cramps.

Understanding Menstrual Cramps: Causes, Symptoms, and Severity Levels

Menstrual cramps are a common experience for many women during their menstrual cycle. For some women, menstrual cramps are mild and short-lived, while for others, they can be severe and debilitating. We'll explore the causes, symptoms, and severity levels of menstrual cramps and discuss how Ayurvedic herbal remedies can help alleviate menstrual pain and discomfort.

Menstrual cramps are caused by contractions in the uterus, which occur in response to the release of prostaglandins. Prostaglandins are hormones that are released during menstruation and are responsible for causing the uterus to contract, which helps to shed the uterine lining. However, when the levels of prostaglandins are too high, they can cause excessive and painful contractions, leading to menstrual cramps.

Symptoms of Menstrual Cramps

The symptoms of menstrual cramps can vary from woman to woman. Some women may experience only mild discomfort, while others may experience severe pain. Common symptoms of menstrual cramps include:

- Pain in the lower abdomen, back, and/or thighs
- Nausea and/or vomiting
- Diarrhea or constipation
- Headaches
- Dizziness or fainting

Severity Levels of Menstrual Cramps

1. **Mild menstrual cramps**: Mild menstrual cramps are characterized by a dull, achy pain in the lower abdomen, which can last for a few hours or up to a day.

2. **Moderate menstrual cramps**: Moderate menstrual cramps are characterized by more intense pain in the lower abdomen and back, which can last for several days.

3. **Severe menstrual cramps**: Severe menstrual cramps are characterized by intense pain that can interfere with daily activities, and can last for several days. Severe menstrual cramps can also be accompanied by nausea, vomiting, and fainting.

Ayurvedic Herbal Remedies for Menstrual Cramps

Ayurveda is an ancient Indian system of medicine that uses herbs and natural remedies to treat various health conditions. Ayurvedic herbal remedies can be an effective way to alleviate menstrual pain and discomfort. Here are some Ayurvedic herbal remedies that can help:

1. **Ginger:** Ginger is a natural anti-inflammatory and can help reduce menstrual cramps. You can add fresh ginger to your tea or take it in supplement form.
2. **Fennel:** Fennel is another natural anti-inflammatory that can help reduce menstrual cramps. You can add fennel seeds to your tea or take them in supplement form.
3. **Cinnamon:** Cinnamon is a natural antispasmodic and can help reduce uterine contractions. You can add cinnamon to your tea or take it in supplement form.

Discomfort During Periods

In addition to menstrual cramps, many women experience discomfort during their period like bloating, fatigue, and headaches

1. **Heat therapy:** Applying heat the lower abdomen can help to relax the muscles and reduce cramps. You can use a heating pad or take a warm bath.
2. **Gentle exercise:** Gentle exercise, such as yoga or walking, can help to improve blood flow and reduce cramps.

Constipation during Periods:

Constipation is a common issue during periods. This can be caused by hormonal changes, dehydration, and a lack of physical activity. Constipation can be uncomfortable and can worsen your menstrual cramps. To manage constipation, it's important to stay hydrated, eat a fiber-rich diet, and engage in regular physical activity.

Menstrual cramps are a common occurrence for many women during their menstrual cycle. The severity of these cramps can vary from mild to severe, and the symptoms can include pain, discomfort, and other issues such as constipation. Understanding the causes and severity levels of menstrual cramps are essential to managing discomfort during periods.

Mind-Body Techniques for Pain Management: Yoga, Meditation, and Acupuncture

I understand how frustrating it can be to feel like nothing is helping to alleviate the pain. That's why I'm excited to share some natural remedies with you that have worked wonders for me. We'll discuss three mind-body techniques that can help manage menstrual cramps

Yoga for Menstrual Cramps

Yoga is a holistic healing practice that can be incredibly beneficial for managing menstrual cramps. Certain yoga poses can help relieve tension in the body and promote circulation to the pelvic area, which can help reduce cramps. Here are some poses that I find helpful for menstrual cramps:

1. Seated Forward Bend (Paschimottanasana): Sit on the floor with your legs extended in front of you. Inhale and reach your arms overhead, then exhale and fold forward, reaching for your feet. This asana helps to calm the nervous system, reducing stress and anxiety that can exacerbate menstrual cramps.

2. Supine Twist (Supta Matsyendrasana): Lie on your back and draw your right knee up toward your chest. Cross your right knee over your body to the left side, and extend your right arm out to the side. This asana helps to release tension in the lower back and hips, easing menstrual cramps and promoting relaxation.

3. Cat-Cow Pose (Marjaryasana-Bitilasana): Begin on your hands and knees, with your wrists directly under your shoulders and your knees directly under your hips. Inhale and arch your back, lifting your tailbone, and gaze toward the ceiling. Exhale and round your spine, tucking your chin to your chest, your pelvis in and abdomen in. This asana helps to massage the

internal organs, promoting circulation and reducing menstrual cramps.

4. Extended Triangle Pose (Utthita Trikonasana): Begin standing with your feet wide apart. Turn your left foot in slightly and your right foot out 90 degrees. Inhale and reach your right arm up toward the ceiling, then exhale and reach your right hand toward your right foot. This asana helps to stretch the hips and relieve tension in the lower back, reducing menstrual cramps.

5. Legs Up the Wall Pose (Viparita Karani): Sit with your left side against a wall, then swing your legs up the wall as you lie back on the floor. This asana helps to improve circulation and reduce swelling, which can contribute to menstrual cramps.

6. Reclining Bound Angle Pose (Supta Baddha Konasana): Lie on your back with your knees bent and the soles of your feet together. Let your knees fall open to the sides

and extend your arms overhead. This asana helps to open the hips and pelvis, reducing tension and cramping in the lower abdomen.

Feel free to enhance your yoga practice by using yoga blocks and pillows for added comfort. Modify and adapt the asanas to your needs, creating a space where your body feels supported and empowered.

Holistic Healing with Meditation

Meditation is a powerful tool for managing menstrual cramps. It can help reduce stress and tension in the body, which can contribute to cramps. Here's a simple meditation practice that you can try:

1. Find a quiet space where you won't be disturbed.
2. Sit comfortably with your spine straight and your hands on your knees.
3. Close your eyes and begin to focus on your breath. Take deep, slow breaths in through your nose and out through your mouth.
4. As you breathe, visualize yourself in a peaceful, relaxing place. This could be a beach, a forest, or anywhere that makes you feel calm and at ease.
5. Continue to breathe deeply and focus on this visualization for several minutes.

Acupuncture for Menstrual Cramps

Acupuncture is an ancient Chinese healing technique that involves inserting thin needles into specific points on the body.

It can help balance the body's energy flow and reduce inflammation, which can contribute to menstrual cramps. Here's what you can expect during an acupuncture session:

1. You'll meet with a licensed acupuncturist, who will ask you about your symptoms and medical history.
2. You'll lie down on a table, and the acupuncturist will insert thin needles into specific points on your body.
3. You may feel a slight pinch or pressure, but the needles shouldn't be painful.
4. The acupuncturist will leave the needles in place for about 20-30 minutes, and you'll be encouraged to relax and breathe deeply.

Breath-work for Menstrual Cramps

In addition to yoga poses, breath-work can be a powerful tool for managing menstrual cramps. Deep breathing can help reduce stress and tension in the body, which can alleviate cramps. Here are some breathing techniques that you can try:

1. Abdominal breathing: Place one hand on your abdomen and take slow, deep breaths, focusing on expanding your belly as you inhale and contracting it as you exhale.
2. Alternate nostril breathing: Using your thumb and ring finger, close off one nostril and inhale deeply through the other nostril. Then, close off the other nostril and exhale through the first nostril. Repeat on the other side.

Meditation for Menstrual Cramps

Meditation is a practice that involves focusing the mind on a particular object, thought, or activity to achieve a state of mental clarity and calmness. It has been shown to be an effective way to manage menstrual cramps by reducing stress and tension in the body. Here are some meditation techniques that you can try:

1. Guided meditation: A practice where a narrator or teacher leads you through a calming journey, helping you cultivate mindfulness, relaxation, and inner peace through their soothing guidance.
2. Body scan meditation: This meditation involves scanning the body from head to toe, focusing on each body part, and noticing any tension or discomfort.

Dietary and Nutritional Strategies: Foods and Supplements that Can Help Alleviate Menstrual Cramps

I've found that making dietary and nutritional changes can greatly alleviate the pain and discomfort associated with menstrual cramps. Let's discuss the foods and supplements that can help manage menstrual cramps, including Ayurvedic herbs, seed cycling, and avoiding certain fast foods, MSG, environmental pollutants, and pesticides.

Ayurvedic Herbs

Ayurveda is an ancient Indian system of medicine that has been used for thousands of years to treat a variety of health conditions, including menstrual cramps. Some Ayurvedic herbs that are commonly used to manage menstrual cramps include ashwagandha, shatavari, and ginger. Ashwagandha is an adaptogenic herb that can help reduce stress and anxiety, which can reduce menstrual cramps. Shatavari is a hormone-balancing herb that can help regulate the menstrual cycle and alleviate cramps. Ginger is a natural anti-inflammatory agent that can help reduce the pain and inflammation associated with menstrual cramps.

Seed Cycling

Seed cycling is a dietary technique that involves consuming certain seeds during different phases of the menstrual cycle to balance hormones and alleviate menstrual cramps. During the follicular phase (days 1-14 of the menstrual cycle), flax seeds and pumpkin seeds are consumed to promote estrogen production. During the luteal phase (days 15-28), sesame seeds and sunflower seeds are consumed to promote progesterone production. By balancing hormones in this way, menstrual cramps can be alleviated.

Let's dive into the specific nutritional benefits of the seeds involved in seed cycling and why they're so beneficial for hormone balancing and overall good health.

Lignans

Flax seeds and sesame seeds are sources of lignans, which are precursors to phytoestrogens. Phytoestrogens can help regulate estrogen levels in humans, and in particular they may inhibit estrogen levels from getting too high in the luteal phase.

Zinc

Pumpkin and sunflower seeds are sources of zinc, which increases production of follicle stimulating hormone (FSH), which triggers ovulation and the production of progesterone so zinc is naturally progesterone boosting.

Iron

Pumpkin and sesame seeds are sources of iron which is important for energy and nervous system health, and as it's lost in menstrual blood, it's important to replenish your iron store each cycle.

Manganese

A strong antioxidant that's essential for bone health and thyroid function. Manganese is found in all seeds, but pumpkin seeds are a particularly good source.

Vitamin E

Pumpkin and sunflower are sources of this powerful antioxidant that boosts progesterone and corrects progesterone-estrogen imbalances.

Selenium

Sunflower seeds are one of the best food sources of selenium, which is important for cognitive function, heart health, thyroid health, and is a powerful antioxidant. Selenium is also found in sesame seeds.

Fast Food, MSG, Environmental Pollutants, and Pesticides

These contribute to hormonal imbalances and exacerbate menstrual cramps. Fast food is typically high in unhealthy fats, sugars, and salt, which can disrupt hormone production and increase inflammation. MSG, a common food additive, can also disrupt hormone production and contribute to inflammation. Environmental pollutants and pesticides can disrupt hormone production and can be found in non-organic fruits and vegetables. To manage menstrual cramps, it's important to avoid these foods and opt for organic, whole foods instead.

Heat Therapy and Hydrotherapy: Using Heat and Water to Relieve Menstrual Cramps

When it comes to managing menstrual cramps, heat therapy and hydrotherapy can be incredibly effective and soothing natural remedies. Let's explore the benefits of using heat and water to alleviate menstrual cramps, as well as some different ways to incorporate these therapies into your menstrual wellness routine.

How Heat Therapy Relaxes Muscles

When we experience menstrual cramps, it's due to the contraction of the uterus. Heat therapy works by relaxing the muscles in the uterus as well as the surrounding muscles in the abdomen and back. When we apply heat to our bodies, it increases blood flow and oxygen to the affected area, which helps reduce pain and inflammation. Heat also helps to stimulate the release of endorphins, our body's natural pain relievers, which can help to ease discomfort and promote relaxation.

Different Ways to Use Heat Therapy for Menstrual Cramps

1. Hot water bottle or heating pad: One of the most common ways to use heat therapy for menstrual cramps is to apply heat to the lower abdomen or lower back with a hot water bottle or heating pad. Simply fill the hot water bottle with warm water or heat up the heating pad and place it on the affected area. You can leave it on for up to 20 minutes at a time and repeat as needed.

2. Warm bath or shower: Taking a warm bath or shower can also be an effective way to ease menstrual cramps. The warmth of the water helps relax the muscles in the body and can help to alleviate pain and discomfort. You can also add essential oils or Epsom salts to your bath for added relaxation and pain relief.

3. Warm compress: Another way to use heat therapy for menstrual cramps is to create a warm compress. Simply

soak a towel in warm water, wring it out, and place it on your pelvis , thighs, or back. You can leave it on for up to 20 minutes at a time, and repeat as needed.

Hydrotherapy: Using Water to Alleviate Menstrual Cramps

Hydrotherapy, or the use of water to promote healing and wellness, can also be an effective way to manage menstrual cramps. Here are a few different ways to incorporate hydrotherapy into your menstrual wellness routine:

1. Warm bath with Epsom salts: Adding Epsom salts to a warm bath can help to relax the muscles in the body, and can also help reduce inflammation and pain. Epsom salts contain magnesium sulfate, which can help promote relaxation and ease tension.

2. Contrast hydrotherapy: Contrast hydrotherapy involves alternating between hot and cold water to stimulate blood flow and reduce pain and inflammation. You can do this by placing your feet in hot water for a few minutes and then switching to cold water for a few minutes. Repeat this process several times.

3. Swimming: Swimming can be a great way to promote relaxation and ease menstrual cramps. The buoyancy of the water can help relieve pressure on the body, and the movement can help stimulate blood flow and promote relaxation.

Aromatherapy and Essential Oils: Benefits and Precautions

I will delve into the benefits and precautions of aromatherapy and essential oils for managing menstrual cramps, but first let's understand how aromatherapy works.

Aromatherapy uses essential oils to enhance your physical and emotional well-being. The molecules in the essential oils enter our bodies through the nose and then travel through the bloodstream, affecting various organs and systems, including the limbic system, which is responsible for our emotions.

When we inhale essential oils, the scent molecules travel through the nose and stimulate the olfactory nerves. These nerves then send signals to the brain, triggering various reactions, including the release of chemicals such as endorphins and serotonin, which are natural painkillers and mood enhancers.

Essential Oils for Menstrual Cramps

Several essential oils are known for their pain-relieving and muscle-relaxing properties, making them useful for managing menstrual cramps. Some of the best essential oils for menstrual cramps include:

1. Clary sage oil: This oil is known for its antispasmodic properties, making it effective in reducing menstrual cramps. Clary sage oil can also help balance hormones and reduce anxiety and stress levels.

2. Lavender oil: Lavender is well-known for its calming and relaxing properties. It can help reduce muscle tension and

relieve pain, making it useful for managing menstrual cramps.

3. Peppermint oil: Peppermint oil is a natural analgesic, which means it can help reduce pain. It also has cooling properties, making it useful for reducing inflammation and muscle tension.

4. Rosemary oil: Rosemary oil is known for its analgesic and antispasmodic properties, making it effective in reducing menstrual cramps. It can also help improve blood flow, which can help alleviate menstrual pain.

Essential Oils to Avoid

While essential oils can be useful for managing menstrual cramps, some oils should be avoided, especially during pregnancy or if you have certain medical conditions. Some essential oils to stay away from include:

1. Sage oil: Sage oil can stimulate contractions and should be avoided.

2. Wintergreen oil: Wintergreen oil contains a high concentration of methyl salicylate, which can be toxic when absorbed in large quantities. It should be avoided by people with aspirin allergies or asthma.

3. Cinnamon bark oil: Cinnamon bark oil can be irritating to the skin and mucous membranes and should be used with caution.

Precautions for Using Essential Oils

When using essential oils for menstrual cramps, it's important to follow some precautions to ensure your safety and the effectiveness of the oils. Here are some essential oil precautions to keep in mind:

1. Always dilute the essential oil before applying it to your skin. You can use a carrier oil such as coconut oil, almond oil, or jojoba oil.
2. Conduct a patch test before using any new essential oil to ensure you don't have an allergic reaction.
3. Use essential oils in moderation. Excessive use of essential oils can lead to toxicity, allergic reactions, or skin irritation.

Aromatherapy with essential oils is a natural and effective way to manage menstrual cramps. The use of essential oils can help relieve pain, reduce muscle tension, and improve your emotional state. However, it's important to use essential oils with caution and follow the proper precautions to ensure your safety and the effectiveness of the oils.

Topical Applications and Massage Therapy: Using Oils, Balms, and Massage Techniques to Ease Menstrual Cramps

When I first started looking for natural remedies to manage the pain and discomfort, I discovered the power of topical applications and massage therapy. I will share my knowledge on how to use oils, balms, and massage techniques to ease menstrual cramps.

DIY Balms and Oils

One of the most effective ways to use essential oils is by making your own DIY balms and oils. Here's how to make your own menstrual cramp balm:

Ingredients:

- 1/2 cup coconut oil
- 1/4 cup beeswax pellets
- 1/4 cup shea butter
- 20 drops of clary sage essential oil
- 15 drops of lavender essential oil
- 10 drops of peppermint essential oil
- 5 drops of ginger essential oil

Instructions:

1. Melt the coconut oil, beeswax pellets, and shea butter in a double boiler until they are fully combined.
2. Remove from the heat and let the mixture cool for a few minutes.
3. Add the essential oils and stir well.
4. Pour the mixture into small jars or tins and let it cool completely.
5. Apply the balm to your lower abdomen and massage it gently into your skin as needed.

Another effective oil blend for menstrual cramps is a combination of clary sage, lavender, and chamomile essential oils. Simply mix a few drops of each oil with a carrier oil such as coconut oil or almond oil and massage into your lower abdomen.

Massage Therapy

Here are some massage techniques that have worked well for me:

1. Abdominal Massage: Lie down on your back and use your fingertips to massage your lower abdomen in a circular motion. Apply gentle pressure and work in a clockwise direction.
2. Acupressure: Apply pressure to the acupressure points located on your lower back and inner ankle. You can use your fingers or a massage ball to apply pressure for a few minutes.
3. Lower Back Massage: Ask a partner or a massage therapist to massage your lower back with firm pressure, working out any knots or tension.

Topical applications and massage therapy can be incredibly effective in easing menstrual cramps. By making your own DIY balms and oils, you can tailor the recipe to your specific needs and preferences. Don't be afraid to experiment with different oils and massage techniques until you find what works best for you. Remember to always listen to your body and seek medical advice if your cramps are severe or accompanied by other symptoms.

Chapter 9

Hormone Disruptors in Young Women: The Impact of Modern Lifestyle Practices

In the hustle and bustle of modern life, we ladies have to deal with countless lifestyle factors that could throw our hormones out of whack. Think birth control pills, poor awareness of toxins, EMF, masculine energy, and binge eating processed junk food, caffeine, and booze. All these can send our bodies into chaos and disrupt their natural balance.

Oral Contraceptives

"Oral contraceptives can be seen as a "quick fix" solution for preventing pregnancy, but they come with potential long-term consequences."

Hormonal birth control may seem like a convenient and easy solution for preventing unwanted pregnancies, but it can have lasting effects on the body's hormonal balance. These synthetic hormone-containing medications can lead to a range of side effects, including changes in mood, weight gain, and irregular periods.

Toxins and endocrine-disrupting chemicals

Toxins and endocrine-disrupting chemicals are present in a variety of household products, from cleaning supplies to personal care items. These chemicals can be found in items we use every day, such as plastic containers, food packaging, and even our drinking water.

One example of an endocrine-disrupting chemical is bisphenol A (BPA), which is found in many plastics, including those used for food storage and water bottles. BPA can mimic the effects of estrogen in the body, disrupting hormonal balance and potentially leading to health issues such as infertility, breast cancer, and thyroid disorders. It is important to look for BPA-free products when shopping for household items.

Another endocrine-disrupting chemical to be aware of is phthalates, which are often used in personal care items such as shampoo, lotion, and fragrance. Phthalates can disrupt the endocrine system by mimicking hormones like estrogen and testosterone, leading to hormonal imbalances and health issues such as obesity, diabetes, and infertility. Look for phthalate-free products when shopping for personal care items.

Triclosan is another common endocrine-disrupting chemical found in antibacterial soaps, toothpaste, and other personal care items. It can disrupt thyroid function and has been linked to hormonal imbalances and antibiotic resistance. Opt for products without triclosan and consider using natural alternatives for hand sanitizing and cleaning.

When it comes to household cleaning products, many contain endocrine-disrupting chemicals such as alkylphenols, which are commonly used in detergents. These chemicals can disrupt hormonal balance and have been linked to reproductive issues in both men and women. Look for cleaning products that are labeled as "green" or "eco-friendly," or make your own using natural ingredients like vinegar and baking soda.

Toxins and endocrine-disrupting chemicals are pervasive in our environment and can have serious effects on our hormonal health. By being aware of the chemicals present in our household products and opting for natural alternatives, we can take steps to reduce our exposure and maintain a healthy hormonal balance.

Limiting EMF Exposure: Managing Our Tech Habits

In today's digital age, technology has become an integral part of our daily lives, and the use of electronic devices has skyrocketed. From smartphones to laptops to Wi-Fi routers, we are surrounded by electromagnetic fields (EMFs). These EMFs emit low-level radiation that can potentially harm our health, especially our hormonal balance. Although we cannot avoid using technology entirely, we can manage our tech habits and limit our exposure to EMFs.

Turn Off and Unplug

One of the easiest ways to reduce our exposure to EMFs is to turn off and unplug our electronic devices when we're not using them. This simple habit can help reduce the amount of radiation we're exposed to on a daily basis. Many of us have a habit of leaving our devices on standby, but this can still emit EMFs that can affect our health. So, it's essential to turn off and unplug your devices when you're not using them, especially before bedtime.

Use Wired Connections

Using wired connections instead of Wi-Fi is another way to limit our exposure to EMFs. Wi-Fi emits EMFs that can be harmful to our health, especially if we're exposed to them for extended periods. If possible, use a wired connection for your internet needs, such as Ethernet cables. Also, avoid placing your Wi-Fi router near your bed, and turn off the Wi-Fi when you're not using it.

Reduce Screen Time

Spending too much time on electronic devices can not only affect our hormonal balance but also disrupt our sleep patterns, leading to other health problems. So, it's essential to take breaks from your devices and spend some time outdoors or doing other activities that don't involve electronic devices.

Manage Your Tech Habits

Managing our tech habits is crucial for our health, especially for our hormonal balance. Although it's impossible to avoid using technology entirely, we can take steps to limit our exposure to EMFs. By turning off and unplugging our devices when not in use, using wired connections instead of Wi-Fi, and reducing our screen time, we can take control of our exposure to EMFs and minimize potential health risks. So, let's manage our tech habits and stay healthy!

Hormonal Imbalances in Women - Causes from Masculine Traits

As young women, we are often encouraged to adopt more masculine traits to succeed in the workplace and in life. However, what many people fail to recognize is that this can lead to hormonal imbalances and impact our overall health and well-being.

Masculine Energy and Its Impact on Hormones

When we adopt masculine traits, we are often encouraged to be more competitive, aggressive, and assertive. While these traits can be beneficial in certain contexts, they can also lead to imbalances in our hormones. In particular, they can impact our levels of estrogen and testosterone, two hormones that play a crucial role in our reproductive health.

Estrogen is a hormone responsible for the development and regulation of the female reproductive system. It helps maintain the thickness and elasticity of the vaginal walls and regulates the menstrual cycle. Testosterone, on the other hand, is primarily responsible for the development of male sexual characteristics, but women also have small amounts of testosterone that help maintain muscle mass and bone density.

When we adopt masculine traits, we can cause imbalances in our estrogen and testosterone levels, which can lead to a range of health issues. These imbalances can result in irregular periods, acne, mood swings, and even infertility.

Identifying Masculine Energy

It's important to be able to recognize when we are exhibiting masculine energy and how it may be impacting our hormonal balance. Masculine energy can manifest in a range of ways, including:

1. Competitiveness: constantly striving to be the best and outperform others
2. Aggressiveness: being confrontational and argumentative

3. Assertiveness: being dominant and overconfident in all situations
4. Emotional suppression: repressing emotions in order to appear strong and in control

Competitiveness can manifest itself in a desire to win at all costs, often putting ourselves under immense pressure to be perfect. This can lead to high levels of stress, anxiety, and a general feeling of being overwhelmed. It can also result in imbalances in estrogen and testosterone levels, leading to irregular periods and decreased sex drive.

Aggressiveness can cause conflict and tension in our relationships, which can be a significant source of stress. It can also lead to a constant state of fight or flight, which can cause imbalances in cortisol, a hormone responsible for managing stress. This can lead to a range of health issues, including weight gain, high blood pressure, and an increased risk of heart disease.

Assertiveness is often seen as a positive trait, but when taken to the extreme, it can become toxic. When we are overly dominant and confident, we can come across as arrogant and dismissive of others' opinions. This can result in a lack of trust and respect in our relationships, which can cause stress and anxiety. It can also lead to imbalances in estrogen and testosterone levels, impacting our reproductive health.

Emotional suppression is a common trait among women who adopt more masculine energy. We often feel the need to repress our emotions to appear strong and in control. However, this can lead to a range of mental health issues, including depression and anxiety. It can also impact our hormonal balance, as repressing emotions can lead to imbalances in estrogen and testosterone levels.

Finding a Healthy Balance

While it's important to be assertive and confident, it's equally important to find a healthy balance between assertiveness and femininity. This means embracing our emotions, expressing ourselves authentically, and valuing collaboration and community over competition. By doing so, we can maintain a healthy hormonal balance and optimize our overall health and well-being.

The Impact of Hormonal Imbalance on Menstruation and Fertility

As a women's health enthusiast, I know firsthand the importance of understanding hormonal imbalances and how they can affect both menstruation and fertility. I will delve into the impact of hormonal imbalances on the female reproductive system and explore some potential solutions.

How Hormones Affect Menstruation

The menstrual cycle is regulated by a complex interplay of hormones, including estrogen, progesterone, follicle-stimulating hormone (FSH), and luteinizing hormone (LH). Any disruptions in the balance of these hormones can result in irregular periods, heavy bleeding, or missed periods altogether.

For example, low levels of estrogen can lead to vaginal dryness, mood swings, and irregular periods. High levels of estrogen, on the other hand, it can cause breast tenderness, bloating, and heavy bleeding.

Progesterone is another key hormone in the menstrual cycle and is responsible for thickening the lining of the uterus in preparation for pregnancy. Low levels of progesterone can result in a short luteal phase, which can make it more difficult to conceive. High levels of progesterone, however, can cause symptoms such as bloating and mood swings.

How Hormones Affect Fertility

Hormonal imbalances can also have a significant impact on fertility. For example, polycystic ovary syndrome (PCOS) is a common hormonal disorder that can cause irregular periods and make it more difficult to conceive. PCOS is characterized by high levels of androgens (male hormones) and insulin, which can disrupt ovulation and affect the quality of eggs.

Thyroid disorders, such as hypothyroidism or hyperthyroidism, can also affect fertility by disrupting the balance of thyroid hormones. Hypothyroidism can cause irregular periods and low levels of progesterone, while hyperthyroidism can lead to a short luteal phase and an increased risk of miscarriage.

Solutions for Hormonal Imbalances

If you suspect that you may have a hormonal imbalance, it is important to seek medical advice. Your doctor may recommend blood tests or ultrasounds to assess your hormone levels and may suggest treatments such as hormone replacement therapy or fertility medications.

In addition to medical treatments, there are also several lifestyle changes that can help balance hormones naturally. For example, regular exercise, a balanced diet, and stress management techniques such as yoga or meditation can all help regulate hormones and improve fertility.

Hormonal imbalances can have a significant impact on both menstruation and fertility. By understanding the role of hormones in the female reproductive system and seeking medical advice when needed, we can take steps to balance our hormones and optimize our health. Remember, every woman's body is different, so it is important to listen to your own body and work with your healthcare provider to find the best solutions for you.

Taking Control: Natural Remedies and Lifestyle Changes for Hormonal Balance

Before we dive into natural remedies and lifestyle changes, let's first understand what causes hormonal imbalances. Hormonal imbalances can be caused by a variety of factors, including stress, poor nutrition, lack of exercise, and environmental toxins. These imbalances can manifest in a variety of ways, including irregular periods, mood swings, acne, and weight gain.

Holistic and Ayurvedic Lifestyle Practices

1. Yoga and Meditation: Practicing yoga and meditation can be incredibly beneficial for hormonal health. These practices can help reduce stress, which is a major contributor to hormonal imbalances. Yoga poses such as

the child's pose, the downward dog, and the bridge pose can help stimulate the endocrine system and promote hormonal balance. Meditation can help calm the mind and reduce stress, which in turn can help balance hormones.

2. Ayurvedic Diet: Following an Ayurvedic diet can help balance your hormones by providing your body with the nutrients it needs to function properly. Foods such as ghee, turmeric, ginger, and cumin can help reduce inflammation in the body and promote hormonal balance. It is also important to avoid processed foods and sugar, which can contribute to hormonal imbalances.

3. Herbal Supplements: Herbal supplements such as ashwagandha, maca root, and vitex can help balance hormones and alleviate symptoms of hormonal imbalances. These supplements should be taken under the guidance of a healthcare provider.

4. Environmental Changes: Making changes to your environment can also help balance your hormones. Avoiding exposure to environmental toxins such as BPA, phthalates, and pesticides can help reduce the risk of hormonal imbalances. Choosing natural cleaning products, personal care products, and cookware can also be helpful.

5. Self-Care Practices: Self-care practices such as getting enough sleep, practicing gratitude, and spending time in nature can also be beneficial for hormonal health. Getting enough sleep is especially important, as it allows the body to rest and repair itself, which can promote hormonal balance.

Hormonal imbalances can be frustrating and debilitating, but there are natural remedies and lifestyle changes that can help bring your body back into balance. By incorporating holistic and Ayurvedic practices into your daily routine, you can take control of your hormonal health and improve your overall wellbeing. Remember to always listen to your body and seek medical advice if you are experiencing severe symptoms or if you are unsure about any of the natural remedies or lifestyle changes.

Chapter 10

Embracing the Journey: Celebrating Your Femininity

Every woman is unique and special, and I'm here to help you embrace your femininity and explore how to honor it. Let us learn how to work with your natural body rhythms and cycles and how to use them to your advantage. We will explore the many ways in which you can honor your femininity and grow into a more self-aware and empowered woman.

Understanding Your Feminine Energy: What Is Femininity and How Can You Embrace It?

The feminine energy is a powerful and beautiful force that can be harnessed to create meaningful connections, creative projects, and inner peace. It is the energy of receptivity and the power of creation. Feminine energy is the source of life, love, and fertility, and it is the key to unlocking your highest potential. As a woman, understanding and embracing your feminine energy is essential to living your fullest life.

The feminine energy can be seen in many forms, from the nurturing mother to the passionate romantic. It is often associated with beauty, grace, creativity, and emotion. It is not a one-size-fits-all definition, as femininity can look different to different women. What is important is to explore your individual feminine energy and how it can be expressed.

No matter what type of woman you are, there are ways to embrace and honor your feminine energy. Start by recognizing and valuing your unique strengths and gifts. Spend time exploring what makes you feel empowered and fulfilled. Take the time to nurture yourself and practice self-care. Develop meaningful connections with other women and appreciate the beauty of your feminine nature.

Embracing your femininity means being comfortable in your own skin, celebrating your unique gifts, and allowing yourself to be vulnerable and creative. It is a journey that requires courage and commitment, but the rewards of being in touch with your feminine energy are immeasurable. As you continue to explore and discover what it means to be a woman, you will find that you become more confident, powerful, and content with yourself and your life.

Honoring Your Body: Practicing Self-Love and Self-Care During Your Cycle

As women, we have the power to honor and respect our bodies in ways that nourish and serve us. Our menstrual cycle can be seen as an opportunity to tune in to our body's needs and take time for ourselves. Learning to appreciate and care for our bodies during our cycle is an essential part of developing self-love and self-care. As we honor our cycle, we can create meaningful rituals that help us feel empowered and connected to our bodies.

When we honor our bodies and the natural rhythms of our cycle, we can use our energy to our highest and best potential. Self-care during our cycle can be a powerful tool to help us connect with our bodies, minds, and souls. Self-care during the cycle is an opportunity to nurture ourselves, take extra time for reflection, and nurture the connection with our intuition.

You can try these simple tips to increase your feminine energy

1. Be mindful of your body's signals and respond accordingly. Pay attention to your physical and emotional needs and honor them.
2. Aim for balance in your life. Make sure to get enough rest, eat healthfully, and exercise regularly.
3. Incorporate self-care activities into your routine. This can include taking a warm bath, reading a book, meditating, or spending time in nature.
4. Journal your thoughts and feelings throughout your cycle. Writing can be a great tool for expressing emotions and processing difficult experiences.
5. Avoid comparing your experience to others. Everyone's bodies and cycles are unique.
6. Seek support if needed. Talk to friends, family, or a therapist if you are struggling with your cycle.

No matter what phase of your cycle you're in, it's important to remember to show yourself some love. Honor your body and all that it is capable of. Self-care and self-love are essential to living a healthy and balanced life, and your cycle is a reminder of the power you possess. Celebrate it.

Moving with Intention: Incorporating Exercise and Movement Into Your Routine

A healthy exercise routine doesn't have to be complicated or time consuming. Even on busy days, it's important to find time to move with intention. Start your day with a few minutes of stretching or gentle yoga to get your body ready for the day. Take a walk during your lunch break, or take your dog for a walk after dinner. If you have the energy, add in a quick home workout or a 10-minute HIIT session. Be mindful of how your body is feeling and adjust your workout accordingly. For example, during certain points of your menstrual cycle, you may need a more restorative or calming practice like Yin yoga to help balance your hormones. Incorporating exercise and movement into your daily routine will help optimize your physical and mental wellbeing.

Having a regular exercise routine is an essential part of any woman's overall health. Not only does it help to keep your body in shape, but it also improves your mental health and can even help with your period cycle. Incorporating exercise and movement into your period cycle can be a great way to stay active, reduce stress, and keep your hormones in balance.

In the **first phase of your cycle**, Rest and recovery activities are essential for women. These activities can help to reduce stress, improve energy levels, and promote overall health and wellbeing. Some examples of activities include yoga, meditation, massage therapy, acupuncture, taking a hot bath, or shower, getting enough sleep, and eating a balanced diet. Additionally, engaging in light physical activity such as walking, gardening, or practicing savasana can help reduce stress and improve mood. By taking time to rest and recover during the first phase of your cycle, you will be better able to manage daily life challenges with ease.

As you move into the **follicular phase**, you'll want to focus more on strength training. This is the time to get in some weight lifting and bodyweight exercises. This will help to increase your muscle strength and tone, which can help to relieve menstrual cramps and reduce your risk of developing chronic pain. Try focusing on bodyweight exercises like squats, lunges, and planks.

When you enter the **ovulatory phase**, it's time to focus on cardio exercises. This is the time to get your heart rate up and your blood flowing. You can try high-intensity interval training (HIIT) or even go for a run or long bike ride. This type of exercise will help increase your energy levels and give you a sense of accomplishment.

Once you enter the **luteal phase**, it's time to slow down. This is the time to focus on low impact exercises such as walking, yoga, or stretching. These activities will help to reduce stress and anxiety, as well as reduce your risk of developing chronic pain. By incorporating exercise and movement into your period cycle, you'll be able to stay active, reduce stress, and keep your hormones in balance. So, make sure to include exercise and movement into your period cycle each month, and you'll be sure to reap the benefits.

Cultivating Healthy Relationships: Creating Boundaries and Connecting with Others

Cultivating healthy relationships is essential for a woman's overall wellbeing, especially when it comes to her menstrual cycle health. Establishing boundaries with others and connecting with them in meaningful ways can help women to manage their stress levels, enjoy meaningful exchanges, and ensure their physical and mental health.

Creating boundaries is the first step in developing healthy relationships. This can include setting limits on how much time is spent with friends and family and how much personal information is shared. It also means being mindful of how much energy is invested in each interaction. This will help reduce stress levels as well as prevent burnout. In addition, boundaries allow for meaningful conversations and exchanges to take place, as each person can arrive with a clear understanding of what they can and cannot expect from one another.

Try our recommendation for Creating safe boundaries

1. **Communicate your needs**: When setting boundaries in relationships, it's important to be clear about what your needs are. For example, if you need more rest during your menstrual cycle, let your partner know in advance and be prepared to answer any questions they may have.

2. **Set boundaries**: To cultivate a healthy relationship, it's necessary to establish boundaries. For example, let your partner know that it's okay to talk to you about your period cycle health, but also let them know that it's not okay to make jokes or belittle your experience.

3. **Respect your body**: When it comes to your period cycle health, it's important to prioritize your own needs and respect your body. For example, if you're feeling exhausted and need some extra rest during your cycle, take time for

yourself and don't feel like you have to do everything your partner wants.

4. **Connect with other women:**Connecting with other women who have similar experiences can be invaluable for understanding your own period cycle health. For example, try joining an online support group or taking a class that focuses on women's health.

5. **Practice self-care:** It's important to take care of yourself during your period cycle health. For example, try journaling, taking a bath, or reading a book to soothe your mind and body during this time.

Practical Tips for Enhancing Your Feminine Energy and Harnessing the Power of the Moon Cycle

It is no secret that women's natural energy and strength are closely connected to the moon's cycles. The monthly lunar cycle has been linked to feminine energy, and many women feel the effects of the moon's power on their emotions, physical and spiritual health. We will explore practical tips for enhancing your feminine energy and harnessing the power of the moon cycles to bring balance and harmony to your life. You will learn how to align yourself with the energy of the phases of the moon, use the moon's guidance to support your health and wellbeing, and create rituals to honor your menstrual cycle. By connecting with your feminine energy and tapping into the power of the moon, you can transform your life and unlock your true potential.

The moon has been a powerful symbol of the Feminine since ancient times. Throughout the ages, women have sought to honor, connect, and nourish the Feminine by creating rituals that are in tune with the moon's cycles. Moon rituals are a unique and powerful way to tap into and enhance your feminine energy. I'll suggest ways to use moon rituals to honor your menstrual cycle and connect with your inner wisdom, so that you can live a life of vibrant health and wellbeing.

Try Our Self Care Moon Rituals

1. **Moon Bathing**: Spend at least 10 minutes each night outside under the moonlight. Take in the beauty of the night sky and absorb the healing energy.

2. **Moon Meditation**: Find a comfortable place to sit and take a few deep breaths. Focus on your breathing and allow yourself to relax. Visualize the moon above you and imagine the light of the moon filling your body with positive energy.

3. **Moon Journaling**: Take some time to reflect on the moon's energy and your own emotions. Write down any thoughts, feelings, or ideas that come to you.

4. **Moon Rituals**: Create a special ritual to honor the moon. You could light candles, burn incense, or create a sacred altar.

5. **Lunar Affirmations**: Write down positive affirmations that are meaningful to you. Read them aloud and repeat them to yourself throughout the day.

6. **Connect With Nature:** Spend time outdoors and connect with nature to absorb the moon's energy. Take a walk in the park or along the beach.

Chapter 11

Recipes

Mindful eating is an approach that combines physical nourishment with emotional awareness. It encourages us to become aware of our thoughts, feelings, and sensations in order to make conscious choices about what we eat and when we eat it. By becoming mindful of our food choices, we create an opportunity for self-care that can help us feel more connected with our bodies and better understand our individual needs. You will learn simple recipes that can be incorporated into your daily life so that you can begin making healthier food choices with ease. Additionally, I'll provide guidance on how to best manage cravings throughout each phase as well as tips for creating a balanced meal plan tailored specifically for you.

I hope that you will have a better understanding of how mindful eating can help support a healthy hormonal balance throughout your monthly cycle as well as gain insight into how to nourish yourself physically and emotionally during each phase.

The Menstrual Phase

1. **Roasted Broccoli with Turmeric**: This dish is a great source of magnesium, which helps to regulate hormones and reduce cramps. It also contains Vitamin K, Vitamin C, and folate, which are essential for a healthy menstrual cycle.
2. **Lentil Soup**: Lentils are a great source of iron, protein, dietary fiber, Vitamin B6 and magnesium—all of which can help ease menstrual symptoms such as cramping or fatigue.

3. **Sweet Potato Fries**: Sweet potatoes are loaded with beta-carotene (which the body converts into Vitamin A) and are an excellent source of potassium both important for maintaining good hormone balance during the menstrual cycle.

4. **Dark Chocolate**: Dark chocolate contains antioxidants that can help reduce stress levels and boost mood during the menstrual phase, plus it's delicious!

Lutel Phase

1. **Roasted Tofu with Avocado Salsa**: This delicious meal is packed with essential nutrients and minerals that are needed during the luteal phase. Tofu is a great source of omega-3 fatty acids, which can help reduce inflammation and support hormone balance. The avocado salsa adds healthy fats, fiber, and vitamins A, C, K, and E.

2. **Lentil Stew with Sweet Potatoes**: This hearty stew is full of fiber-rich lentils that help stabilize blood sugar levels and keep energy levels up during the luteal phase. Sweet potatoes provide additional fiber as well as vitamin A for hormone balance.

3. **Millet Salad with Broccoli and Chickpeas**: This light yet filling salad is loaded with nutrients that are beneficial during the luteal phase. Millet provides protein, iron, magnesium, zinc, folate, and B vitamins for energy production while broccoli provides antioxidants to protect cells from damage caused by free radicals. Chickpeas are a good source of fiber to help maintain healthy digestion as well as zinc for immune system support.

5. **Methi leaves and Butternut Squash Soup**: This comforting soup is packed with nutrients that are beneficial during the luteal phase. Methi leaf is a great source of saponins and antioxidants, which help reduce cholesterol, vitamins A and C, folate, and iron for hormone balance. Butternut squash provides beta-carotene for healthy skin and vision as well as magnesium for energy production.

Follicular Phase

1. **Roasted Vegetable Millet Bowl**: This hearty vegetarian bowl is packed with protein, fiber, and minerals like iron, magnesium, and zinc. Roast a variety of vegetables such as sweet potatoes, zucchini, bell peppers, onions and mushrooms in olive oil until golden brown. Toss cooked millet with the roasted vegetables and top with a drizzle of tahini for added flavor.

2. **Lentil Curry**: This easy-to-make lentil curry is loaded with essential vitamins and minerals like folate and iron. Start by sautéing garlic and onion in coconut oil or ghee until golden brown. Add spices like turmeric, cumin, coriander powder to the mix before adding cooked lentils to the pan. Simmer until all the flavors combine then serve over a bed of steamed basmati rice for an extra boost of energy-boosting complex carbohydrates!

3. **Avocado Toast**: Avocados are rich in healthy fats that can help keep your hormones balanced during the follicular phase of your cycle. Toast whole grain bread then top it with mashed avocado seasoned with salt and pepper for a simple yet delicious meal that's full of nutrients!

4. **Spinach Omelet**: A spinach omelet is an excellent source of iron, protein, zinc, and magnesium, which are all essential for a healthy follicular phase. It's also high in vitamins A and C, which can help keep your skin looking youthful during this time of the month.

5. **Yogurt Parfait**: Greek yogurt is packed with calcium to help strengthen your bones during this time of the month, as well as plenty of protein to keep you feeling full longer throughout the day. Topping it off with some fresh fruit will give you additional vitamins such as vitamin C needed for a healthy follicular phase too!

Ovulatory Phase

1. **Lentil Soup with Spinach**: Cook lentils in vegetable broth until tender then add spinach to the soup until wilted. Serve hot topped with Parmesan cheese for added flavor and calcium, which is important for reproductive health during ovulation.

2. **Greek Yogurt Parfait**: Layer plain Greek yogurt with fresh berries or other fruit of choice along with chopped nuts or seeds like chia or hemp hearts for added protein and healthy fats that are beneficial during this time of the cycle.

3. **Zucchini Noodles with Pesto**: Spiralize zucchini noodles, then top them with pesto sauce made from fresh herbs like basil or parsley. The iron in Zucchini helps support fertility health during ovulation.

My Favorites

I'm sure you've heard it before, but eating healthy is the key to a happy and healthy life. But what if I told you that eating healthy doesn't have to be boring or tasteless? That's right - with my favorite recipes, you can enjoy delicious meals that are packed with essential nutrients and minerals. I will share some of my favorite recipes that have helped me regulate my hormones. From breakfast ideas to dinner dishes and even snacks in between, Not only will these recipes help keep your body in balance, but they are also incredibly tasty! With simple step-by-step instructions and plenty of nutritional information included, I'm sure you'll find something that fits.

Lentil Soup

Ingredients:

2 tablespoons coconut oil

1 onion, diced

3 cloves garlic minced

1 teaspoon coriander powder

1 teaspoon cumin powder

6 cups vegetable broth or water

1 cup red lentils rinsed & drained

½ teaspoon turmeric

¼ teaspoon cinnamon

¼ teaspoon pepper powder (optional)

Salt & pepper to taste

Instructions:

1.) Heat coconut oil in a large pot over medium high heat. Add onions & cook for about 5 minutes or until softened then add garlic & coriander and cumin powder & cook for another minute or two until fragrant.

2.) Pour in vegetable broth then add lentils & spices (turmeric, cinnamon & pepper powder). Bring the mixture to a boil then reduce heat to low so it's just gently simmering with the lid slightly askew (to allow steam to escape). Simmer for 20 minutes or until lentils are tender but not mushy - stirring occasionally throughout the cooking time if needed!

3.) Remove from heat then season with salt & pepper before serving hot with crusty bread or bed of rice on the side! Enjoy!

Millet Salad with Broccoli and Chickpeas

Ingredients:

2 cups cooked millet of your choice

1 cup cooked chickpeas

1 cup broccoli florets, chopped into small pieces

1/4 cup Coconut oil

2 tablespoons fresh lemon juice

2 cloves garlic, minced

1/2 teaspoon sea salt

Freshly ground black pepper, to taste

Instructions:

1. In a large bowl, combine the cooked millet, chickpeas and chopped broccoli. Set aside.
2. In a small bowl, whisk together the coconut oil, lemon juice and garlic until combined. Season with salt and pepper to taste.
3. Pour the dressing over the millet mixture and toss to combine until everything is evenly coated in dressing. Serve immediately. Enjoy!

Urad Dal Porridge

Ingredients:

1 cup split urad dal (black gram)

3 cups water

2 tablespoons jaggery, grated or chopped

1/4 teaspoon ground cardamom

1/4 teaspoon ground nutmeg (Optional)

2 tablespoons gingelly oil

1 tablespoon grated Coconut

Instructions:

1. Soak the split urad dal in 3 cups of water for at least 1 hour. Drain and rinse the dal.

2. Place the soaked and drained dal in a medium saucepan and add 3 cups of fresh water. Bring to a boil over high heat, then reduce the heat to low and simmer for 5-7 minutes, stirring occasionally, until the dal is soft and creamy.

3. Add jaggery, cardamom, nutmeg and gingelly oil to the cooked dal and stir until combined. Simmer for an additional 5 minutes over low heat until all ingredients are well blended together.

4. Add grated coconut during the last few minutes of cooking time for added sweetness and texture. Serve warm with extra gingelly oil if desired

Rava Dosa and Coconut Chutney

Ingredients for rava dosa

2 cups rava/sooji

1 cup wheat flour/ atta

1 teaspoon cumin seeds

1 teaspoon crushed black pepper

2 tablespoons chopped coriander leaves

Salt to taste

3 tablespoons ghee or coconut oil for cooking the dosa

Instructions for rava dosa

1. In a large bowl, mix together the rava, flour, cumin seeds, black pepper powder and salt.
2. Add enough water to make a thick batter and mix well until no lumps remain.
3. Heat a nonstick pan over medium heat and grease it with some ghee or oil.
4. Pour a ladleful of the batter onto the pan and spread it out in a circular motion to make a thin dosa.

5. Drizzle some ghee around the edges of the dosa and cook for 1 minute or until golden brown on both sides.

Ingredients for coconut chutney

½ cup fresh grated coconut

4 green chilies (or to taste)

¼ teaspoon mustard seeds

¼ teaspoon cumin seeds

3 tablespoons roasted chana dal (bhuna chana)

2 tablespoons tamarind paste

1 tablespoons coconut oil

4 curry leaves

1 dry red chili

Salt to taste

Instructions for coconut chutney

1. In a blender, add coconut, green chilies, cumin seeds, roasted chana dal and tamarind paste along with 2 tablespoons of water and blend into a smooth paste.

2. Transfer this mixture into a bowl and add salt as per your taste preferences; mix everything together well.

3. Add coconut oil for tempering one hot add mustard seeds, curry leaves and dry chili add this to your coconut paste and mix until combined properly.

4. Serve this delicious coconut chutney with hot dosas or idlis!

Cycle based Diet Plan

OPTION 1

	BREAKFAST	LUNCH	DINNER	SNACK
MENSTRUAL	Urad Dal porridge Poha Roasted Broccoli with Turmeric	Lentil Stew Curd Rice Sambar	Ragi Dosa Coconut rice & Avial Idly & Sambar	Herbal Tea Rava Dosa Onion Pakoda
OVULATORY	Pesarattu Rava Dosa & Coconut chutny Appam	Zucchini Noodles with Pesto Coconut Rice & Avial Rasam Rice	Masala Dosa Lentil Soup with Spinach Uttapam	Yoghurt parfait Dahi Vada Steamed Back Channa
LUTEAL	Appam with Coconut Milk Pongal & Sambar Urad Dal porridge	Aloo Gobi Chana Masala Vegetable Biryani	Bhindi Masala Gujarati Kadhi Rasam Rice	Aloo Tikki Chaat Rava Dosa Roasted Nuts
FOLLICULAR	Pesarattu & coconut Chutny Urad Dal porridge Spinach Omelette	Sambar rice & Vegetable Pongal Dal Makani	Lentil Curry Channa Masala Panner Masala	Avocado Toast Dokhla Aloo Cutlets

Cycle based Diet Plan

OPTION 2

	BREAKFAST	LUNCH	DINNER	SNACK
MENSTRUAL	Ginger Turmeric Smoothie Protein Smoothie Quinoa Porridge	Turmeric Tofu Scramble Veggie Lentil Tacos Lentil Burger	Lentil Stew Sweet Corn Soup Veggie-loaded Quiche	Herbal Tea Chia Balls Turmeric Popcorn
OVULATORY	Matcha Green Smoothie Sweet Potato Toast & Avocado Mushroom Frittata	Stuffed Bell Peppers Tofu & Veggie Fajitas Mushroom Risotto	Grilled Veggie Skewers Spicy Tofu Tacos Lentil Soup with Spinach	Yoghurt parfait Almond Butter & Banana Hummus with Rice Crackers
LUTEAL	Buckwheat Bowl Breakfast Burrito Baked Oatmeal & Apples	Quinoa Stuffed Zucchini Boats Veggie StirFry & Rice Buddha Bowl	Lentil Bolognese Pasta Lentil Shepherd's Pie Roasted Veggie Wrap	Turmeric Ginger Tea Dark Chocolate & Almonds Pumpkin Seed Balls
FOLLICULAR	Veggie Scramble Wrap Acai Bowl Lentil Breakfast Bowl	Bolognese with Zucchini Noodles Rainbow Salad Sweet Potato Tacos	Lentil Curry Veggie & Halloumi Skewers Teriyaki Tofu StirFry	Avocado Toast Berry Smoothie Cucumber & Hummus

Chapter 12

28 Day Smoothie Recipes

As women, we understand that our bodies go through a beautiful dance of hormonal changes each month. It's crucial to nourish ourselves with the right foods to support our well-being and navigate these fluctuations with grace. I'm excited to share with you a collection of delicious and nutrient-packed smoothie recipes carefully crafted to harmonize with your menstrual cycle.

Each recipe is designed with love and tailored to the specific needs of each phase—follicular, ovulatory, luteal, and menstrual. As you sip on these vibrant blends, you'll feel the power of nature's bounty, providing you with essential vitamins, minerals, and antioxidants that promote hormonal balance and overall vitality.

Get ready to embrace the symphony of flavors and textures as you dive into the world of luscious fruits, nourishing greens, and hormone-balancing ingredients. Whether you're looking to boost your energy during the follicular phase, enhance your mood in the luteal phase, or ease menstrual discomfort, we have a smoothie recipe to cater to your unique needs.

So grab your blender, gather your favorite ingredients, and embark on this delicious and empowering journey. Let these 28-day smoothie recipes be your companion as you embrace the flow of your menstrual cycle. It's time to treat yourself to the vibrant colors, delicious flavors, and nourishing benefits of these carefully curated blends. Get ready to sip, savor, and support your hormonal well-being—one smoothie at a time. Cheers to your vibrant health and embracing the magic of your menstrual cycle!

Day 1: Strawberry Banana Smoothie

The Strawberry Banana Smoothie is a delicious and nutritious drink that provides a host of benefits for your health. Strawberries are packed with antioxidants, which help fight inflammation and protect your cells from damage. Bananas are high in potassium, which helps regulate blood pressure and improve heart health. Additionally, bananas are a great source of fiber, which aids in digestion and promotes healthy bowel movements. When combined, strawberries and bananas create a tasty and nutrient-dense smoothie that can be enjoyed as a snack or meal replacement. Drinking this smoothie regularly can help boost your energy levels, support healthy digestion, and improve overall wellness.

Ingredients:

- 1 cup strawberries
- 1 medium ripe banana
- 1 cup almond milk
- ½ cup plain Greek yogurt

Day 2: Mango Lassi Smoothie

Mango Lassi Smoothie: Packed with immune-boosting vitamin C and skin-loving beta-carotene, this smoothie is a delicious and nutritious way to start your day. The mango in this smoothie is high in vitamin C, which helps to support a healthy immune system and promote collagen production for healthy skin. The probiotics in the yogurt can also aid in gut health and digestion, while the turmeric can help reduce inflammation in the body.

This refreshing smoothie is not only tasty but also provides a host of health benefits to keep you feeling your best.

Ingredients:

- 1 ripe mango
- 1 cup plain Greek yogurt
- ½ cup coconut milk
- 1 tsp honey

Day 3: Spinach and Avocado Smoothie

The Spinach and Avocado Smoothie is packed with nutrients that can provide a range of health benefits. Spinach is a great source of vitamins A, C, and K, which can support bone health and immune function. It is also high in iron and folate, which are essential for maintaining healthy blood and preventing anemia. Avocado is a great source of healthy fats, which can help support heart health and improve brain function. It is also high in fiber, which can help promote digestive health and prevent constipation. This smoothie is a great way to start your day with a nutrient-packed breakfast that can provide sustained energy and keep you feeling full and satisfied.

Ingredients:

- 1 cup fresh spinach leaves
- 1 ripe avocado
- 1 cup almond milk
- 1 tbsp honey

Day 4: Apple Cinnamon Smoothie

Apple Cinnamon Smoothie is not only delicious, but also offers a range of health benefits. Apples are a great source of fiber, which can help keep you feeling full and satisfied. Cinnamon has anti-inflammatory properties and may help lower blood sugar levels. This combination can help regulate digestion and prevent blood sugar spikes, making it a great option for those with diabetes or pre-diabetes. Additionally, apples are high in vitamin C and antioxidants, which can help boost your immune system and improve your overall health. The Apple Cinnamon Smoothie is a perfect choice for a healthy and tasty breakfast or snack option.

Ingredients:

- 1 medium apple
- ½ cup plain Greek yogurt
- 1 cup almond milk
- 1 tsp cinnamon powder

Day 5: Papaya Smoothie

Papaya Smoothie: Loaded with enzymes such as papain and chymopapain, papaya smoothie aid digestion and alleviate bloating and constipation. It is also a rich source of vitamin C, which is essential for collagen production and healthy skin. Papaya contains antioxidants like beta-carotene and lycopene, which protect against free radical damage and improve cardiovascular health. Additionally, papaya is rich in potassium, which helps regulate blood pressure and reduce the risk of heart disease. Drinking papaya smoothie on a regular basis can be a delicious and nutritious addition to a healthy diet.

Ingredients:

- 1 medium papaya
- 1 banana
- 1 cup almond milk
- 1 tbsp honey

Day 6: Orange Creamsicle Smoothie

The Orange Creamsicle Smoothie with banana and coconut milk is a delicious and nutritious way to start your day. This smoothie is packed with essential nutrients such as potassium, fiber, and vitamin C, which are all beneficial for your overall health. The banana and coconut milk in the smoothie provide a creamy and satisfying texture while also promoting healthy digestion and improving heart health. Additionally, the orange juice in the smoothie is rich in antioxidants, which can help boost your immune system and improve skin health. Overall, the Orange Creamsicle Smoothie with banana and coconut milk is a tasty and healthy way to fuel your body and start your day on the right foot.

Ingredients:

- 1 medium orange
- ½ cup coconut milk
- 1 cup plain Greek yogurt
- 1 tsp vanilla extract

Day 7: Rose Petal Smoothie

The Rose Petal Smoothie with Banana is a delicious and nutritious way to start your day. This smoothie is rich in antioxidants and has anti-inflammatory properties due to the presence of rose petals. Antioxidants help protect the body against damage from free radicals, which can cause cell damage and lead to chronic disease. The addition of bananas provides a good source of potassium, which is important for regulating blood pressure and maintaining heart health. Additionally, bananas contain fiber, which aids in digestion and helps keep you feeling full throughout the day. The combination of these ingredients makes for a nourishing and tasty smoothie that can provide you with a range of health benefits.

Ingredients:

- 1 cup rose petals
- 1 cup almond milk
- 1 banana
- 1 tbsp honey

Instructions:

1. Wash the rose petals and remove the stem.
2. Add all ingredients in a blender and blend until smooth.
3. Pour into a glass and enjoy

Day 8: Blueberry yogurt Smoothie

Blueberry yogurt smoothie is a delicious and healthy beverage that is packed with numerous health benefits. Blueberries are loaded with antioxidants that protect the body against free radicals and help prevent cellular damage. Yogurt, on the other hand, contains probiotics that promote gut health and boost the immune system. When combined, blueberries and yogurt make a tasty and nutrient-dense smoothie that can improve digestion, enhance bone health, and reduce inflammation. Additionally, blueberry yogurt smoothie is a good source of vitamins and minerals such as vitamin C, vitamin K, calcium, and potassium, which support healthy skin, strong bones, and a healthy heart.

Ingredients:

- 1 cup blueberries
- ½ cup plain Greek yogurt
- 1 tsp vanilla extract
- 1 cup almond milk

Day 9: Pineapple and Ginger Smoothie

The Pineapple and Ginger Smoothie with Coconut Milk is a powerful combination of ingredients that offers a wide range of health benefits. Pineapple is rich in enzymes that aid digestion and reduce inflammation, while ginger is known for its anti-inflammatory properties and ability to ease nausea. Coconut milk is a great source of healthy fats, which can help improve heart health and reduce inflammation in the body. Together, these ingredients create a delicious and refreshing smoothie that can help improve digestion, reduce inflammation, and promote overall health and well-being.

Ingredients:

- 1 cup pineapple chunks
- 1 tbsp chopped fresh ginger
- ½ cup coconut milk
- 1 tbsp honey

Day 10: Beetroot and Carrot Smoothie

The Beetroot and Carrot Smoothie with almond milk is packed with benefits for overall health and wellness. Beetroot is a great source of nitrates, which can improve blood flow and lower blood pressure. It is also high in antioxidants, which can help protect against cellular damage and inflammation. Carrots are rich in beta-carotene, which can improve eye health and boost the immune system. Together, these ingredients create a delicious and nutrient-packed smoothie that can help improve cardiovascular health, boost immunity, and provide a range of essential vitamins and minerals.

Ingredients:

- 1 small beetroot
- 1 medium carrot
- 1 cup almond milk
- 1 tsp honey

Instructions:

1. Peel, chop, and boil the beetroot and carrots until tender.
2. Add all ingredients to a blender and blend until smooth.
3. Pour into a glass and enjoy!

Day 11: Kiwi and Pineapple Smoothie

Kiwi and Pineapple Smoothie with Coconut Milk: Rich in Enzymes and Nutrients for Digestive Health and Immune Support. This delicious smoothie is not only a tasty treat, but it also provides a number of benefits for your digestive health and immune system. The kiwi and pineapple are both rich in digestive enzymes, which can help break down food and improve nutrient absorption. Additionally, both fruits are high in vitamin C, which can help boost your immune system and promote collagen production for healthy skin and hair. The coconut milk adds a creamy texture and provides healthy fats that can support brain function and reduce inflammation. Together, these ingredients make for a refreshing and nutritious smoothie that can help support your overall health and well-being.

Ingredients:

- 2 medium kiwi
- 1 cup pineapple chunks
- 1 cup coconut milk
- 1 tbsp honey

Day 12: Mixed Berry Smoothie

Mixed Berry Smoothie: Packed with antioxidants that support overall health, boost immunity, and reduce inflammation. This smoothie contains a mix of berries such as strawberries, blueberries, and raspberries, which are high in antioxidants like anthocyanins, quercetin, and Vitamin C. These antioxidants help to neutralize harmful free radicals in the body, preventing cellular damage and reducing the risk of chronic diseases like cancer and heart disease. In addition to the antioxidant benefits, the Mixed Berry Smoothie is also a great source of dietary fiber, which can help regulate digestion and improve gut health. The fiber also helps to keep you feeling full and satisfied, making it a great option for a healthy breakfast or snack.

Furthermore, the blend of berries in this smoothie also provides an array of vitamins and minerals, including Vitamin K, folate, and potassium. These nutrients are essential for maintaining healthy bones, reducing inflammation, and regulating blood pressure.

Overall, the Mixed Berry Smoothie is a delicious and nutritious way to start your day or refuel after a workout. Its high antioxidant content, fiber, and essential nutrients make it a powerhouse drink that can support your overall health and well-being.

Ingredients:

- 1 cup mixed berries (strawberries, raspberries, blueberries)
- 1 medium banana
- ½ cup plain Greek yogurt
- 1 cup almond milk

Day 13: Chocolate Banana Smoothie

Chocolate Banana Smoothie: Packed with nutrients to boost energy and mood. Bananas are a great source of potassium, which can help regulate blood pressure and improve heart health. The addition of cacao powder provides a rich source of antioxidants, which can help protect against cellular damage and promote healthy aging. This smoothie also contains almond milk, which is a good source of calcium and vitamin E, both of which are important for bone health and skin health. Overall, this smoothie is a delicious and nutritious way to start your day or refuel after a workout.

Ingredients:

- 1 medium ripe banana
- 1 tbsp cocoa powder
- ½ cup plain Greek yogurt
- 1 cup almond milk
- 1 tsp honey

Day 14: Green Tea Smoothie

Green Tea Smoothie: Packed with antioxidants, which promote overall health and wellbeing. The green tea in this smoothie is also known to boost metabolism, aiding in weight loss and weight management. Additionally, the smoothie's combination of green tea and fruits provides a healthy dose of vitamins and minerals, such as vitamin C, which supports immune system function and helps protect against cellular damage. The smoothie is also rich in fiber, which promotes healthy digestion and can help lower cholesterol levels. Overall, the Green Tea Smoothie is a delicious and healthy way to start your day and support your body's natural detoxification processes.

Ingredients:

- 1 cup green tea
- 1 medium ripe banana
- 1 cup spinach leaves
- ½ cup plain Greek yogurt
- 1 cup almond milk

Instructions:

1. Steep the green tea in freshly boiled water for 5 minutes, then allow it to cool.
2. Combine all ingredients in a blender.
3. Blend until smooth and creamy.
4. Pour into a glass and enjoy!

Day 15: Raspberry and Peach Smoothie

Raspberry and Peach Smoothie: This delicious smoothie is packed with nutrients that are beneficial for your health. The raspberries in this smoothie are a rich source of antioxidants, which can help improve the health of your skin and hair. They also provide vitamin C, which is essential for collagen production, helping to keep your skin looking youthful and radiant. The peaches in this smoothie are also a great source of vitamin C, as well as vitamin A, potassium, and dietary fiber. Together, these ingredients make for a refreshing and nutritious smoothie that will leave you feeling energized and satisfied.

Ingredients:

- 1 medium ripe peach
- 1 cup frozen raspberries
- ½ cup plain Greek yogurt
- 1 cup almond milk

Day 16: Manjal Smoothie

Turmeric smoothies are a great way to incorporate this powerful spice into your diet. Turmeric is known for its anti-inflammatory and antioxidant properties, making it a great addition to any health-conscious individual's diet. When combined with other healthy ingredients, turmeric can help boost your immune system, reduce inflammation, and improve digestion. A turmeric smoothie may also help promote healthy skin and hair, as well as reduce the risk of chronic diseases such as heart disease and cancer. Overall, a turmeric smoothie is a delicious and nutritious way to add some extra health benefits to your daily routine.

Ingredients:

- 1 banana
- 1 tsp turmeric powder or fresh turmeric peeled
- ½ cup plain Greek yogurt
- 1 cup almond milk
- 1 tsp honey

Day 17: Mango and Coconut Smoothie

Mango and Coconut Smoothie: This tropical smoothie is packed with benefits for your health and well-being. Mango is high in vitamin C, which is essential for collagen production, and is also a great source of antioxidants. Coconut milk provides healthy fats and can help boost your immune system. The combination of these two ingredients can help improve digestion, reduce inflammation, and support healthy skin and hair.

Ingredients:

- 1 medium ripe mango
- ½ cup coconut milk
- ½ cup plain Greek yogurt
- 1 tbsp honey

Day 18: Cherry and Almond Smoothie

The Cherry and Almond Smoothie is a delicious and nutritious way to start your day. Cherries are packed with antioxidants, which can help reduce inflammation in the body and boost immunity. Almonds are a great source of protein and healthy fats, which can help keep you feeling full and satisfied throughout the morning. Together, these ingredients make for a creamy and satisfying smoothie that is not only delicious but also provides numerous health benefits. This smoothie can help reduce oxidative stress in the body, which can lead to improved skin health and a more radiant complexion. The vitamin E found in almonds can also help improve hair health and prevent damage. Overall, the Cherry and Almond Smoothie is a delicious and nutritious way to support your health and well-being.

Ingredients:

- 1 cup cherries
- 1 tbsp almond butter
- ½ cup plain Greek yogurt
- 1 cup almond milk
- 1 tsp honey

Day 19: Watermelon and Mint Smoothie

The Watermelon and Mint Smoothie is a refreshing and delicious drink that not only tastes great but also provides numerous health benefits. Watermelon is a low-calorie fruit that is rich in vitamins A and C, both of which are essential for maintaining healthy skin and hair. It is also a good source of lycopene, a powerful antioxidant that can help protect against cancer and heart disease. Mint, on the other hand, is known for its ability to soothe digestive issues and reduce inflammation in the body. When combined, watermelon and mint create a hydrating and nutrient-dense smoothie that is perfect for hot summer days or as a post-workout drink.

Ingredients:

- 2 cups diced watermelon
- 1 tbsp fresh mint leaves
- ½ cup plain Greek yogurt
- 1 cup almond milk

Day 20: Spinach and Pineapple Smoothie

The Spinach and Pineapple Smoothie is a nutrient-dense powerhouse that offers numerous health benefits. Spinach is packed with vitamins and minerals, including vitamin A, vitamin C, iron, and calcium, all of which help support healthy bones, skin, and immune function. Pineapple, on the other hand, is rich in bromelain, an enzyme that aids in digestion and helps reduce inflammation in the body. The combination of these two ingredients makes for a delicious and refreshing smoothie that can help boost your energy levels, support healthy digestion, and provide your body with the nutrients it needs to thrive

Ingredients:

- 1 cup fresh spinach leaves
- 1 cup pineapple chunks
- ½ cup plain Greek yogurt
- 1 cup almond milk
- 1 tsp honey

Day 21: Banana and Peanut Butter Smoothie

Banana and Peanut Butter Smoothie: This delicious smoothie is packed with nutrients that can benefit your body in many ways. Bananas are a great source of potassium, which can help regulate blood pressure and improve heart health. Peanut butter provides healthy fats and protein, which can help keep you full and satisfied throughout the day. Additionally, the combination of banana and peanut butter can help reduce inflammation in the body, which can alleviate symptoms of conditions such as arthritis and asthma.

Ingredients:

- 1 medium ripe banana
- 1 tbsp peanut butter
- ½ cup plain Greek yogurt
- 1 cup almond milk

Day 22: Carrot and Ginger Smoothie

Carrot and Ginger Smoothie: Packed with nutrients like beta-carotene, vitamin A, and vitamin C, this smoothie is great for supporting healthy skin, hair, and eyesight. Carrots are also rich in fiber, which can help support healthy digestion and keep you feeling full. Ginger has anti-inflammatory properties that can help reduce inflammation in the body, which is important for maintaining overall health. Additionally, ginger has been shown to have anti-nausea effects, making this smoothie a great option for those experiencing morning sickness or motion sickness.

Ingredients:

- 1 medium carrot
- 1 tbsp fresh ginger
- ½ cup plain Greek yogurt
- 1 cup almond milk
- 1 tsp honey

Day 23: Strawberry and Chia Smoothie

The Strawberry and Chia Smoothie is not only delicious, but it is also packed with a variety of health benefits. The combination of strawberries and chia seeds provides an excellent source of fiber, which can aid in digestion and promote a healthy gut. Strawberries are also high in vitamin C, which is essential for immune system function and collagen production, leading to healthier skin and hair. Chia seeds are rich in omega-3 fatty acids, which can help reduce inflammation in the body and support heart health. Additionally, the combination of strawberries and chia seeds provides a good balance of protein, carbohydrates, and healthy fats, making this smoothie a great option for a balanced and nutritious breakfast or snack.

Ingredients:

- 1 cup strawberries
- 1 tbsp chia seeds
- ½ cup plain Greek yogurt
- 1 cup almond milk
- 1 tsp honey

Day 24: Papaya and Lime Smoothie

Papaya and Lime Smoothie: Packed with digestive enzymes and vitamin C, this smoothie is great for improving digestion and promoting a healthy immune system. The papaya contains papain, a digestive enzyme that helps break down proteins, while the lime provides vitamin C to boost the immune system and aid in collagen production. Additionally, papaya is rich in fiber and antioxidants, which can help improve gut health and reduce inflammation in the body. Overall, this smoothie is a refreshing and nutritious way to support your overall health and well-being.

Ingredients:

- 1 medium papaya
- 1 tbsp lime juice
- ½ cup plain Greek yogurt
- 1 cup almond milk
- 1 tsp honey

Day 25: Blueberry and Peach Smoothie

Blueberry and Peach Smoothie: Packed with antioxidants and anti-inflammatory properties, this smoothie is a great way to start your day. Blueberries are high in vitamin C, which supports a healthy immune system and collagen production, while peaches are rich in vitamin A, which promotes healthy skin and eyes. Together, they provide a delicious blend of sweet and tart flavors while helping to reduce inflammation, improve digestion, and support overall health and wellness. Additionally, the high fiber content of both blueberries and peaches can help regulate blood sugar levels, making this smoothie a perfect choice for those looking to maintain steady energy levels throughout the day.

Ingredients:

- 1 medium ripe peach
- 1 cup blueberries
- ½ cup plain Greek yogurt
- 1 cup almond milk
- 1 tbsp honey

Day 26: Chikoo Almond Smoothie

Indulge in the creamy sweetness of chikoo paired with the nutty goodness of almond milk. This smoothie is a delightful blend of flavors that not only satisfies your taste buds but also provides a nourishing boost of nutrients. Chikoo, also known as sapodilla, is rich in dietary fiber, vitamins, and minerals, while almond milk adds a dose of healthy fats and a creamy texture to the smoothie.

Ingredients:

2 ripe chikoos (sapodilla)

1 cup almond milk

Optional: honey or maple syrup for sweetness

Day 27: Pineapple and Coconut Smoothie

Pineapple and Coconut Smoothie: This tropical blend is not only delicious but also packed with health benefits. Pineapple is rich in bromelain, an enzyme that helps with digestion and reduces inflammation. It is also a great source of vitamin C, which boosts the immune system and promotes collagen production. Coconut milk contains healthy fats that can improve heart health and provide a sustained source of energy.

spiritual well-being in order to achieve optimal menstrual health.

Over the course of the previous few chapters, we have gained knowledge on how to provide proper nourishment for our bodies by preparing nutrient-dense dishes appropriate for each phase and recipes for 28-day smoothies. By including these items in our diets, we may ensure that our bodies receive the essential nutrients for maintaining good hormonal balance and achieving overall wellbeing.

In general, it is my aim that this book has provided helpful insights and strategies for embracing our femininity, celebrating our bodies, and taking control of our menstrual health and overall wellness. You should always keep in mind that your menstrual period is a normal and wonderful part of your life journey, and you should embrace it with love, acceptance, and gratitude.

About The Author

Vidhya Shanmugam is a pelvic yoga therapist, a successful author, and a devoted wellness coach. She has a strong desire to help women improve their health and prevent illness through holistic practices.

Vidhya is an enthusiastic advocate of Ayurveda, an ancient therapeutic practice that seeks to balance a person's mental, physical, and spiritual well-being. Her own experiences have inspired her to help others through the practice of Ayurveda.

In addition to her work as a health and wellness counselor, Vidhya is also a well respected hatha yoga instructor. She incorporates yoga into her holistic healing practice because she is a staunch believer in its ability to bring about harmony between the physical, mental, and spiritual realms.

Her latest book, "The Holistic Menstrual Guide for Women," is evidence of her commitment to holistic medicine and her mission to give women greater power. In it, she shares her knowledge about the menstrual cycle, alternative treatments, and healthy lifestyle habits.

Vidhya's purpose is to promote intuitive holistic health for women, and Mum21 is her company's core focus. Vidhya's goal, through both her book and her company, is to provide women the information they need to make healthy decisions for themselves.

www.ingramcontent.com/pod-product-compliance
Lightning Source LLC
LaVergne TN
LVHW061614070526
838199LV00078B/7277